Praise for *Jesus and the B*

"In a world that's never been more crowded with noise, do you wonder if you'll ever again find a fresh voice with a new idea, especially about personal spiritual growth? Tempted as I am to keep this discovery to myself and wish you good luck unearthing your own, I learned too much from this book to do that in good conscience. Lori Stanley Roeleveld's Jesus and the Beanstalk: Overcoming Your Giants and Living a Fruitful Life is the antidote to the glut of drivel that masquerades as pious self-help books these days. Do yourself a favor and see how Lori deftly uses humor and uncommon sense to mine biblical truth from an unlikely fairy tale and painlessly nurture you in the process."

—**Jerry B. Jenkins**, *New York Times* best-selling author

"*Brilliant* is an overused word. But I can't help using it to describe *Jesus and the Beanstalk*, because this book is brilliant. The book ticked me off (because it's deeply challenging), stirred hopes I haven't felt for an age (because of how real Roeleveld makes Jesus), and made me nod with an admiring smile (because she perfectly nailed my inner thoughts and questions in ways I hadn't been able to articulate). This is a beat-up book. What I mean is you'll underline, dog-ear, and reread it so often it'll soon remind you of *The Velveteen Rabbit*. Tattered and yet beautiful because it has changed you from your core and is utterly real."

—**James L. Rubart**, best-selling author of *The Long Journey to Jake Palmer*

"*Jesus and the Beanstalk* is no bedtime story. It's a survival guide for Christians living in a land of giants... the type that make us want to hide under the covers. *Jesus and the Beanstalk* is packed with practical insights and scripture that help us become seed-planting, stalk-climbing, stone-slinging, giant-slaying disciples of Christ. You can do this... and you won't be alone. So throw back the covers. Start climbing. There are giants to fight."

—**Tim Shoemaker**, author and speaker

"Christian scholars and apologists have rightly noted that introducing the gospel to the postmodern mind requires a different approach. One such approach is that used by Jesus—it involves story. Jesus' parables were not just cute set pieces to His ministry, but powerful tools for challenging intellectual strongholds and personal paradigms. In *Jesus and the Beanstalk,* Lori Roeleveld not only honors the parable principle, she employs it to great success. Springboarding off the most basic of childhood tales, Roeleveld deconstructs the story of the youthful, adventurous giant-killer into a practical, challenging invitation to spiritual growth. With prose rich in humor and illustration, Roeleveld takes us on a journey through Scripture, fleshing out biblical principles in simple, yet profoundly prophetic ways. A great example of postmodern engagement as well as a fun, insightful, challenging read."

—**Mike Duran**, author of *The Telling*

"In *Jesus and the Beanstalk: Overcoming Your Giants and Living a Fruitful Life,* Lori Roeleveld helps us discover the giant-slaying heritage we have as Jesus followers. Although Christ's powerful arsenal of truth is available to us, we often spend our lives running from the stockpile of weapons, trying to bargain our safety with mere beans. With insight and wisdom, Lori teaches us how to gather slingshot stones for battle and confidently slay the obstacles of our Christian lives."

—**Vonda Skelton**, author, speaker, and founder of Christian Communicators Speakers Training

"Lori Stanley Roeleveld has given us new spiritual and practical motivation for increasing our ministry effectiveness. This book is refreshing and relevant to daily life. Lori weaves creative, practical, and powerful possibilities for us, as disciples to live out our faith through sharing Christ in encouraging ways."

—**Rev. Jim Hollis**, Pastor of Northside UMC and Executive Director at Proactive Ministries

Other books by Lori Stanley Roeleveld

Red Pen Redemption

Running from a Crazy Man (and Other Adventures Traveling with Jesus)

JESUS *and the* BEANSTALK

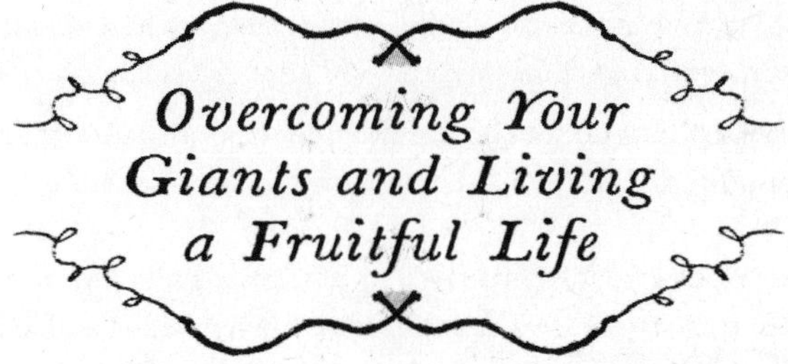

Overcoming Your Giants and Living a Fruitful Life

LORI STANLEY ROELEVELD

Abingdon Press
Nashville

JESUS AND THE BEANSTALK
OVERCOMING YOUR GIANTS AND LIVING A FRUITFUL LIFE

Macro Editor: Holly Halverson

Published in association with Leslie H Stobbe Literary Agency.

To protect the privacy of certain individuals, the names and identifying details have been changed.

Library of Congress Cataloging-in-Publication Data

Names: Roeleveld, Lori Stanley, author.
Title: Jesus and the beanstalk : overcoming your giants and living a fruitful life / Lori Stanley Roeleveld.
Description: First [edition]. | Nashville, Tennessee : Abingdon Press, 2016.
Identifiers: LCCN 2016011738 | ISBN 9781501820045 (pbk.)
Subjects: LCSH: Success—Religious aspects—Christianity. | Jack and the beanstalk—Miscellanea. | Fairy tales—Miscellanea. | Storytelling—Religious aspects—Christianity. | Bible. Peter, 2nd, I, 1-10—Criticism, interpretation, etc.
Classification: LCC BV4598.3 .R655 2016 | DDC 248.4—dc23 LC record available at https://lccn.loc.gov/2016011738

16 17 18 19 20 21 22 23 24—10 9 8 7 6 5 4 3 2 1

MANUFACTURED IN THE UNITED STATES OF AMERICA

To my children, Zack and Hannah:
May you be effective and fruitful in your knowledge of Jesus Christ, and may you topple every giant this side of glory. I can honestly say I will love you forever.

Contents

Contents

Once Upon a Foreword

The woman across the table from me was pleasant, slightly nervous, and seemed uncertain what I would say. We were at a writers conference in North Carolina. She was a conferee, and I was on faculty. At such conferences, time is set aside for attendees to schedule fifteen minutes with a faculty member to ask questions and even get a brief review of their work. This was a critique session, and she had selected me to review her submission. It is an anxious time for conferees. They fear negative comments and long for a word that gives them hope that publication might be in their future. I was happy to tell the woman that she had "the chops" to be a writer.

That woman was Lori Roeleveld, and you hold her third book in your hand. If you haven't already noticed, I was right. Lori has what it takes to write books—meaningful, God-centered books.

It takes more than technique to pen a book such as *Jesus and the Beanstalk*. It takes knowledge, a love for the subject, a love for the reader, and a willingness to draw lessons from personal experiences. It is this kind of book that makes the world of writing noble and meaningful. This is more than just a book. It is a conduit to a better, more meaningful Christian walk. The pressure to be meaningful in a world filled with distracting noise is especially necessary on Christian subjects.

Jesus and the Beanstalk is crafted to touch mind, heart, and soul. It has no lesser goal than to remind all believers that they are giant-killers. In an age when there are many new and frightening affronts to people of faith, there is no better time to be reminded that giants can be felled by faith and determination.

Lori reminds us that there have always been such giants in the lives of Christians, and those giants are not going away any time soon. It is a much-needed message, and readers may, by reading this text, find more steel in their spiritual spines. Lori does this without preaching. She does not occupy a pulpit, nor does she teach from an ivory tower. Instead she walks the same trail as we all do. She does not take a position at the rear of the pack to push us forward, nor does she lead us from the front by pulling us like dogs on a leash. No, she takes her position at the side of the reader and says, "Here is what I know; here is what I've learned; here is why I have confidence in you."

We need theologians to plumb the depths of the Bible and to clarify doctrine. We need preachers to open the Book for daily living and show us the way of worship. But often what we need most is a compatriot, a fellow pilgrim on the road with enough scars to prove, "I have walked this path before."

There is help in this book. There is encouragement. There is motivation. And there is a steady message that God makes all things possible—even in the twenty-first century. There are no sermons in this book, but there is wisdom presented clearly and faithfully. Each chapter offers stones we can use to slay the giants around us as the boy who would be king, David, used to slay Goliath. This makes the book not only devotional and educational but also practical in a fresh and new way.

Lori has, in her ever engaging way, given us something to think about and the kind of encouragement that helps us move forward in the living out of our faith. Using the well-known children's tale "Jack and the Beanstalk" as a backdrop and grounding all of her teaching in a faithful reading of the Bible, Lori takes us on an adventure of thought and faith until we reach a new and stronger determination to defeat the giants that assault our daily lives.

Lori Roeleveld has done us and the kingdom of God a great favor—as you are about to find out.

Alton Gansky
award-winning author of more than 35 books

Why Atheists Fear Fairy Tales

Is it dangerous to read children fairy tales?

This is the question inspired by statements made by leading atheist, author, and evolutionary biologist Richard Dawkins.[1] In a 2014 interview, Dawkins linked a diet of fairy tales with religious beliefs and a rejection of science. Dawkins later retracted his statement and launched a campaign in favor of imagination, but the initial article sparked a rich conversation, especially in a time when many skeptics would say the Christian faith is based on "fairy tales."

There is a connection between faith and fairy tales, but it has nothing to do with rejecting facts and everything to do with having eyes that seek eternal truths. Dawkins was on to something with his original comment. Atheists are right to fear fairy tales. Stories are powerful agents of change. After all, what motivates you to apply God's Word in a meaningful and effective way? Jesus knew that, for most of us, it is story.

Tell us the truth that God is good all the time and we have a fact for our files, a verse to commit to memory, a peg on which to hang our hopes. But tell us an epic story in which a girl encounters a series of trials, a strong, evil opponent, and the temptation to doubt the goodness of God yet still prevails, and we now have material with which our souls can fashion wings. When this everyday hero holds tight to truth and gives flesh to the fact of trusting God's goodness, she inspires us to live a greater story within our own.

False gods are mute. Idols are silent. No one ever received poetry or parables from a statue, a bank account, or a test tube. The living God is a communicator. When he wanted to reach us, he didn't send a digital readout, a lab report, or a thesis on his attributes.

Instead, he told his story through Jesus and showed us how our story intersects with his. He chronicled history, yes, and he recorded facts, it's true; but he also employed parable, irony, word pictures, humor, biography, and prophetic revelation. In addition, he created the heavens and the earth, painted with a lavish, extravagant, artistic hand.

He reaches out to us in every way. Of course, he speaks through the sciences and math. He speaks through dance, films, plays, novels, and arias. God displays a particular passion, though, for story.

He hard-wired us to receive life-changing truth through stories. Songs, films, books, photos, and art that tell stories transport us to his eternal campfire beneath the uncountable stars where he is every hero, every great father, every searchlight, every breathtaking plot twist, and every ending that is simultaneously unexpected and yet inevitable. You just know he enjoys a cliffhanger.

Facts ground us, give us footing, and secure us in place, but stories lift our eyes to meet his gaze. They remind us of our former glory that was lost but is ours again through Jesus.

Once upon a time, there was a perfect God. He created a people to love, placing them in a world he designed only for them. An evil one, seeking to rob God of his joy, tempted them. They chose to rebel against the one who loved them perfectly. The evil one, though, underestimated God's love and inventiveness. God devised a plan to redeem his fallen creation, a way to restore us to relationship with him and to reclaim even creation from the certain condemnation awaiting the tempter.

This story of a love strong enough to sacrifice everything is so rich and glorious it demands we tell it a thousand different ways. This story cries out through creation, through God's written Word, through his living Word, Jesus, and through the expressed imagination of all humanity.

This world will one day pass away along with all the fossil records, calculators, and evolutionary diagrams. Only what's true will remain, and we'll celebrate these truths on the other side. Our stories will survive into eternity. We'll tell them and create new ones forever.

Fairy tales serve a purpose for all ages. My little ones shivered when they heard tales of children in dark forests encountering evil witches, but this instilled in them the truth that evil exists, is powerful, and needs to be overcome. As teenagers, they cheered on Neo, Frodo, and Luke Skywalker, identifying on a soul-affecting level with a solitary hero who remains true even when the world is in upheaval. Moreover, when Thor and Loki wrestle for power and Thor chooses to deny himself for the greater good, my grown-up heart remembers I'm part of a larger story. I'm inspired to deny myself for the sake of honoring my Father and loving others.

Yes, I learn these truths through God's Word. Still, I figure out how to live them through stories because my life is my story and my story is a single thread woven into his epic tapestry.

Atheists fear fairy tales because fairy tales remind mere mortals we aren't the sum of our cells or the weight of our water and DNA. We're not destined for dust, nor did we emerge from goo. We're God-breathed. He ransomed us. We shine like stars in the universe. Our bodies house souls that will soar through the heavens one day if we respond to the call of Jesus Christ.

We are those who will one day walk again with God.

When we do, we'll sing, recite poems, laugh, and weave endless tales. So light the fire, pull up a chair, and let me tell you a story about Jesus and the Beanstalk. Once upon a time, there was a land full of giants. . . .

PART 1

JESUS AND THE BEANSTALK

I am the true vine, and my Father is the vineyard keeper. He removes any of my branches that don't produce fruit, and he trims any branch that produces fruit so that it will produce even more fruit.

John 15:1-2

Part 1 introduces the pathway to effective and fruitful Christian living as described in 2 Peter 1:1-10 and explores how "Jack and the Beanstalk" can help us apply this passage to our lives.

1

Living in a Land of Giants

We live in a world populated with giants.

Giant obstacles to true faith.

Giant barriers to godly lives.

Giant strongholds of sin—in our lives and the lives of loved ones or neighbors. Giant worries. Giant fears. Giant problems such as human trafficking, political corruption, racial division, raising pure children, what to serve for dinner tonight.

So even when we come to Christ, even when we know and love Jesus, even when we know his Word, worship with his people, and pray—we still live in a land populated with giants, and in comparison, we don't stand a chance.

Or do we?

Up Against Giants

In my forties, I studied karate. I was new at it, but I'm competitive. I entered my first tournament as a lowly orange belt. I won first place in two divisions: kata (a series of choreographed moves) and weapons. With only the sparring division left, I felt confident. Sparring occurs when two opponents don protective gear and score points by throwing kicks and punches at each other, making contact without intent to injure. It was in that division I encountered a giant.

I entered the ring for my bout and turned to talk with other students as

I waited for my opponent. When the warning bell rang and I whirled to face her, I was looking square into her belly button. I stood opposite an unnaturally tall, refrigerator-shaped, twenty-five-year-old farmwoman, looking as if she'd trained by hauling small tractors at the county fair. At that precise moment, I lost the bout.

I don't recall much about the actual match except I never moved. I could hear my karate teacher shout, "Do something! Anything! Aw!" It was over with breathtaking speed. Technically my opponent won, but really, I defeated myself the second I contemplated her navel.

Flash forward two years. I faced another giant in a similar karate tournament. I had two more years of training, but I was still outmatched. Again, I opposed a woman who was more skilled, younger, and in better shape. She exuded confidence. But one weapon I'd learned to engage was my mind.

It was clear this girl believed I was no match for her. I might not have been if she'd been prepared for me to come at her like a middle-aged female spinoff of Jackie Chan. I caught her completely off guard by displaying no fear and blitzing her the moment the bell rang. Without hesitation I attacked. I scored two points, and she was so rattled, I managed to sneak in a third to win the match within seconds. There I stood, still the lesser fighter, but now the victor. What changed between my first match and my second is this time I had refused to defeat myself. I might be out-skilled. I might fight out of my league. I might still go down, but I will no longer do the work for my opponents.

We Christians do that though, don't we? In a land of giants, too often we spend so much time contemplating our opponents and weighing the odds, we defeat ourselves. Let me save you some time. The odds are always in favor of the giant—always—but odds don't win battles. Ask David.

God's Word says there are giant forces of evil at work in this age. In Matthew 13, Jesus gave us the parable of the sower and told us the evil one will carry off some of the seed planted in peoples' hearts. In the following parable, he describes an enemy who plants weeds among the good seed in a farmer's field under cover of dark. These stories speak to a relentless, invasive enemy at work in our midst. Battling such pervasive evil will require diligent persistence on our part. There's nothing easy involved in what we're about these days. We face aggressive, abominable giants. We will surely be defeated if we do their work for them!

I hear what you're thinking: we have to face reality. Living in a land populated by giants, we are small, outmatched opponents. That is a fact, the powerful truth. All right, I'll give you that.

Individually we're puny compared to the evil giants at large. Even when we combine forces, we're still small compared to the truly big forces of darkness. Working together can sometimes produce (short-term) a promising start on a magnificent tower, but it doesn't take long for it all to dissolve to babble. Even on our good days, we struggle to get along and stay out of our own way. Not to mention we're frail, sinful, and limited. We mess up. We get sick. We tire. We die. How can we hope to defeat giants?

God Loves Small

There's good news in this too, though, because God loves small. That's right. The great God of the universe is passionate about working small. Consider the biblical proof of this fact.

First, there's a mysterious little verse in Zechariah 4:10: "For whoever has despised the day of small things shall rejoice, and shall see the plumb line in the hand of Zerubbabel. 'These seven are the eyes of the LORD, which range through the whole earth'" (ESV). Now Zechariah was looking at more extensive issues with this verse than our individual consolation when opposing giants. But the sense of it is a warning to beware of writing something off because it starts small. God repeats this theme in numerous Bible stories, so many we can't ignore the truth that Scripture as a whole testifies to God's love of working small.

God didn't make Gideon's army bigger before leading them into battle; he made it smaller (Judges 7). King David was the youngest, the runt of Jesse's litter of sons, but God chose him to succeed Saul as king (1 Samuel 16:1-13).

The Israelites started as a puny, seemingly inconsequential tribe, a fact God relished repeating to them (Deuteronomy 7:6-8). Zacchaeus was so small he had to climb a tree to see Jesus, and yet Jesus singled him out for the gift of his presence (Luke 19:1-10). Five loaves and two fishes were a small offering for thousands of hungry people, and yet, in Jesus's hands, it became an abundant feast (Matthew 14:13-21). Bethlehem is a small city in which to be born (Micah 5:2), and Nazareth was a no-account place to be from, like every other Podunk town from which a person can hail (John 1:46). Yet God chose to grace them with his glory.

One key to facing giants is understanding that God revels in using small people, places, tribes, and churches because, through them, he reveals even more of his glory. Isn't that the point? Not to draw attention to great men, women, tribes, and nations but to draw attention to the Creator God and his plan of redemption.

Small Acts Can Have Big Impact

Imagine a writer coming from a small village in the smallest state and hoping to be of any use in furthering the kingdom of God. How would such a small-town girl even think God might notice her and use her for his glory? Yet God has given even this minor author great stories to tell.

When I started blogging, I knew my friends read my work, along with my family. After several months, my readership grew to about thirty readers a day. It didn't get much higher for years except for occasional flurries of activity. Even now, I don't have a large readership compared to those of major bloggers. When I petition the heavens about this and slip my complaint into God's suggestion box, he whispers a reminder: I don't have to be big to be of use to him. Sometimes I pout about that because, boy, those big numbers come in pretty handy down here. But I'm learning to see things from his perspective.

For example, God sometimes uses my small blog to affect others whose numbers are more impressive. Best-selling authors, filmmakers, and bloggers with greater audiences have read my posts and let me know a post influenced them. In this way, God multiplies the impact of my small blog, as he multiplied the impact of Ananias.

Ananias understood feeling small. We don't read much about him in Scripture. Several short verses in Acts 9 describe how he received instructions from God to go to "Judas' house on Straight Street" and lay hands on a certain man (v. 11). Ananias was understandably daunted because he knew the man God sent him to heal was aggressively persecuting followers of Jesus. Out of obedience, Ananias went to Saul, laid hands on him, and influenced the man who would become the apostle Paul. Ananias had to affect only one person in order to have a part in changing the world. If we embrace this truth, it will free us to find the courage to obey when God sends us to our Straight Street.

One night, a blogger in Aurora, Colorado, with a (then) small audience, commented on a post I wrote that she was thinking of giving up writing. Afterward, she attended a movie with her teenage daughters. They were sitting in theater 9 to see *The Dark Knight Rises* when James Eagan Holmes shot into the crowd. Ironically, my post had been about how some people will always choose evil. The next day, this woman wrote a post about God's protection—a post that went viral. Although up until then she'd had only a few readers, hundreds of thousands read this post. We never know the day God will hand us the story he wants to reach many, so we must remain faithful to the everyday few.

God further illustrated the nonissue of my small beginning in March of 2014. I wrote a post about a news report that the government of North Korea had sentenced a group of Christians to execution. My post explored the question of what difference their deaths would make to us in the West. How would we live differently knowing North Korean believers face prison, torture, and death? I posted the essay, sent the e-mail out to my modest group of followers, and went on with my day.

That evening, I chatted online with another author while I checked my blog numbers for the day. "That's funny," I messaged Aaron, "a post I wrote today had over three thousand views. Wow, I've never had that happen!"

We continued chatting, and Aaron urged me to check the stats again.

"Guess what," I responded. "It's up to eight thousand views. What's going on?"

God taught me a lesson that day about what he can do when he wants a message to fly. Over the next three days, readers viewed that post over one million times, and today, people are still reading it. Several months later, readers shared one of my posts so many times it went viral over Facebook. The numbers of readers for those posts defy their starting place. No one who knew my daily following would have predicted that any single post could reach that wide of an audience, but God loves to reveal himself by using those of us who are small in big ways. If he can use this little-known writer, he can use you, loved one.

We live in a land populated by giants to which we are small in comparison, but God loves taking what is small and glorifying himself through smallness. Who dares despise the day of small things? Not I. When I'm tempted to despise my smallness, I resist because I know my size isn't what matters. God's vision of me is the only important thing.

There's a second reason we have every reason to hope even though we live in a land of giants: we come from a long line of giant-killers. We'll explore that truth in the next chapter.

Small Steps Toward Slaying Giants

1. List the giants in your life. List the problems, people, habits, and barriers overwhelming you. Then add the giants you wouldn't even imagine you could take on—maybe diabetes, racial reconciliation, or human trafficking. What feelings surface as you compile this list?
2. Read the story of Gideon in Judges 6–7, taking special note of Judges 7:2. Why is it good for us, as well as for God's glory, for God to work using those of us who are small?
3. Keep track this week of all the times you feel incapable, insignificant, or as if you will never make a difference. What would happen next week if each time you felt that way, you thanked God that he sees you, praised him for his greatness, and intentionally focused on his power instead of your own limitations?
4. Look at the list of giants you've compiled. Is any one of those too great for God? After you read the name of each giant, read 1 John 4:4. Ask God for the faith to believe, in a life-altering way, what he says in that verse.

❧ ❧ ❧

One Stone for Your Sling: The odds are always in favor of the giant—always—but odds don't win battles. Ask David.

2

A Long Line of Giant-Killers

We live in a land populated by giants, and we are small in comparison. But we have hope, first, because God loves taking what is small and glorifying himself through smallness.

Second, we come from a long line of giant-killers.

Scripture documents our lineage. What we know to be true is that if we have come to Christ, God adopts us into his family and, therefore, we share his family tree. So even if you're like me and don't come from a family steeped in missionaries, ministers, and upstanding citizens, you still have a worthy heritage, one that includes giant-killers.

Lack of Lineage

My parents have worked hard to contribute to their community and to honor God, but you need look back only as far as my grandparents' generation to find strange and ornery human beings. Honestly, my family tree is laden with fruits and nuts. I remember bringing homework to the corner store my grandfather owned and asking him, the butcher, what I should write in the blank about our family heritage. "What are we, Gramp? Italian? Irish? English?"

"Swamp Yankee," he told me, gesturing with a raw hotdog. "You put down we're Swamp Yankee." This is the New England equivalent of the Clampetts on *The Beverly Hillbillies*. The next day, my teacher shook her head and told me to take my work home again, this time to ask my mother. (When my grandchildren ask about our heritage, I plan to tell them to write, proudly, Swamp Yankee.)

Another time, as I shopped yard sales with my mother and aunt, I encountered a large, oily, one-armed man who greeted me with great enthusiasm. He embraced me and exclaimed how healthy I looked. I was accustomed to running into odd characters related to us, so I endured the awkward display. When the man left, I turned, expecting to hear our connection to him. "Who was that?" my mother asked.

"What do you mean, who was that?" I said, horrified. "Aren't we related?"

They shook their heads. Then my aunt asked, "If you didn't know him, why did you let him hug you?"

"He looked strange enough to be family, that's why!"

This shady lineage troubled me as a child. In school, I read stories of great families, people with long lines of upstanding ancestors with rich histories. I wished I'd had a noble, commendable ancestry.

So when I came upon Hebrews 11, which lists Noah, Abraham, Sarah, and more, I recognized the opportunity to come from something, to belong to a great line, to find identity in the context of a rich heritage of faith.

Heritage of Giant-Killers

This is the heritage we share, you and I. If we follow Christ, have received his forgiveness, and have been a recipient of his grace, then we are sisters and brothers in the family of God. We inherit this incredible legacy of faith. Here, in God's Word, those who came before us faced giants and found, by the grace of God, strength to defeat them. So can we.

When Moses sent twelve spies into the Promised Land, ten returned with the report that there were giants in the land—with large, walled cities. Caleb and Joshua, however, were giant-killers by faith. Their response after spying the land: "We can totally take those giants." (Admittedly, that's a paraphrase, but if you read Numbers 13, you'll agree that it sums it up.)

Of course you know about David, who, when he heard Goliath calling out the nation of Israel, responded like the giant-killer he was about to reveal himself to be: "And David said to the men who stood by him, 'What shall be done for the man who kills this Philistine and takes away the reproach from Israel? For who is this uncircumcised Philistine, that he should defy the armies of the living God?'" (1 Samuel 17:26 ESV). Absorb those giant-killing words!

Consider that when Jesus arrived on the planet, the nation of Israel was feeling particularly small, surrounded as they were by the giants of Rome, the Pharisees, and their own bitterness. Jesus, however, took on the giant prince of this world and made his redemptive plan clear to us. You, of course, remember he inhabited our smallness to do so (Philippians 2:5-7). Furthermore, in John 14:12, he promised we would do greater things than he: "I assure you that whoever believes in me will do the works that I do. They will do even greater works than these because I am going to the Father."

What's Our Problem?

We have within us the potential to be giant-killers. The Bible teaches this, and even when we forget it, we testify to it by populating our culture with tales of small heroes toppling giants. It's as if deep within our DNA God planted a reminder of our giant-killing heritage, and it surfaces in the stories we tell, the fairy tales we create, the movies we produce, and the longings we try to quiet when we're feeling especially small. Our original calling remains.

Let's recap. We live in a land full of giants and we're small, but God loves using small things to bring glory to himself. Furthermore, we come from a long line of giant-killers.

These things are true. I know you agree. So, here's my question for you. What exactly is our problem? Why isn't our problem where to bury all the dead giants? Why aren't we having workshops on how to dodge falling giants? Why aren't there more celebrations over their demise?

I can see two reasons, which I'll explore next. A fairy tale explains one reason. God's Word explains the other.

Small Steps Toward Slaying Giants

1. C. S. Lewis says this about fairy tales: "When I was ten, I read fairy tales in secret and would have been ashamed if I had been found doing so. Now that I am fifty, I read them openly. When I became a man I put away childish things, including the fear of childishness and the desire to be very grown up."[1] What's your opinion of fiction and its role in the Christian life? How have stories affected you?
2. When you were growing up, what was your favorite fairy tale or bedtime story? For some of us, our dearest stories played out on movie screens. What was your best-loved movie? What are the themes of the story that came to mind, and why is it meaningful to you?
3. What movies or stories do you treasure now? List ten and see if you find common themes. What does that tell you about your own story? Reread Hebrews 11 and think about being part of this line. How does that change your perception of your potential?
4. In Mark 4:10-12, Jesus explains the reason he uses parables. Is there one that stands out for you? What does this say about their importance in furthering the kingdom of God?
5. C. S. Lewis also wrote, "My Dear Lucy, I wrote this story for you, but when I began it I had not realized that girls grow quicker than books. As a result, you are already too old for fairy tales, and by the time it is printed and bound, you will be older still. But some day you will be old enough to start reading fairy tales again."[2] Are you ready to start reading fairy tales again?

One Stone for Your Sling: It's as if deep within our DNA God planted a reminder of our giant-killing heritage, and it surfaces in the stories we tell, the fairy tales we create, the movies we produce, and the longings we try to quiet when we're feeling especially small.

3

A Fairy Tale and a Promise from God

Why aren't we more effective at toppling giants?

We live in a land full of giants. We're small, but we know God loves using small things to bring glory to himself. We come from a long line of giant-killers. What exactly is our problem? Why aren't people stepping over more fallen Goliaths?

I have two thoughts.

Jack's Mother's Viewpoint

The first reason we aren't toppling more giants is that the world doesn't see us as giant-killers. Too often we view ourselves, and our faith, through the eyes of those who don't believe. To others, those of us who follow Jesus look like Jack in "Jack and the Beanstalk."

Jack and his mother lived in a land during a time of great famine. They were poor and hungry. They made do until all they had left of value was a single, dry milk cow. Jack's mother sent him out to sell the cow at market, but he returned with only a handful of beans.

To Jack's mother, those beans appeared worthless—better to have kept the cow. In disgust, she tossed them from the window, demanding Jack go back to retrieve old Bessy. The beans disappeared into the earth. The twist, of course, was that they were magic beans. A great vine erupted from the earth, one that would lead Jack to discover he was capable of toppling giants.

Isn't this how the world sees the Christian faith, much as Jack's mother saw those beans? The world values cows: sacred cows, cash cows, and actual cows. Without a Christ-informed perspective, we naturally value only what we can see, hear, smell, touch, taste, or trade for goods at the nearest big-box store. We value what makes sense in this world, in this moment, at this time.

What Faith Sees

When we trade our reliance on what the world values for the gift of Jesus Christ, when we tell others we've found something of greater worth than our cows, something that contains the very power of life, the power to transform ordinary people into giant-killers—all they see is a handful of worthless beans. If we view our faith through their eyes, that is all we see as well, and that outlook affects the way we live.

For years I suffered serious health problems. My doctor diagnosed me with systemic lupus erythematosus. Lupus is an autoimmune disease considered chronic and sometimes disabling. Specialists told me to expect a shortened lifespan and disability by middle age, and they said not to plan on birthing children. (With medical advances, many doctors today would probably not give a lupus patient this kind of prognosis.) Chronic illness had a significant impact on my life.

Despite concerns about my ability to conceive, in 1989, I gave birth to a son and, in 1993, a daughter. Shortly after Hannah was born, I spent a night in prayer (being up with the baby anyway). During this prayer time, I felt led to request healing. I'd asked for healing before, but this time it seemed inspired not only by my own longing but also by the prompting of the Holy Spirit. I didn't feel anything special following the prayer, and yet gradually, over months, my symptoms disappeared, my health was restored, and my days became illness-free. I've now been without symptoms for over two decades.

The next time I visited my doctor, I told him I believed God healed me. "People don't heal from lupus," he said. "You're in remission." After ten years of "remission," he begrudgingly admitted that I appeared healed. He occasionally mentions lupus as a possible source of an ache or a pain. I've learned to simply state, "I don't have lupus, so there must be another source." There always is.

It would be easy to see myself through his eyes. I could live as if at any moment I might become horribly ill again. If I did, I might find myself acting as if I am sick when actually I'm well. It's hard to exercise the courage to insist God healed me. I know in the doctor's eyes and even in the eyes of some other Christians, it's an odd thing to credit God's work through prayer for eradicating an incurable disease. Still, here I am.

Discouraged by Others

Likewise we can allow people around us to convince us we aren't giant-killers. What we read in God's Word, hear taught in our faith community, and understand through prayer inspires us to act. When we tell others what we're about, some will try to discourage us—like Jack's mother—to hurry back to town and see if we can recoup our cows.

I've watched friends face this discouragement from family when they shared a vision of entering the mission field, leaving a lucrative job for ministry, or starting a local outreach to tough neighborhoods. I've seen it happen to people defending biblical values, choosing to forgive people whom others would abandon, or attempting to make changes in their lives that others imagine impossible to make.

We can be discouraged and tempted to abandon the life to which God has called us by agreeing to view our situations through Jack's mother's eyes or the eyes of the people around us who don't follow Jesus. This evil tactic has sidelined me, and many others. We're still Christians, still love Jesus, still have the promise of eternal life, but we feel (and often are) less effective and productive than we could be. The remedy for this, as Peter tells us in 2 Peter 1:1-10, is to look again at our handful of beans. (More on this in a few pages.)

Powerful, Living God

Be clear. There's nothing "magic" about our faith, as the world views magic. Our faith has power because we have placed it in a powerful, living

God. He's not a force we conjure, and our prayers aren't spells. We don't have a Tinkerbelle God who exists only because we believe. We aren't practitioners of Christianity but rather followers of the person, Jesus, who is God.

When, however, we exercise our faith, when we put it into practice through obeying God's Word and trusting him to work, the results are powerful, mesmerizing, and supernatural. Miracles occur. Transformations happen. Giants fall. The impossible becomes possible, the unloving learn to love, and the blind see. That's better than magic; that's effective, fruitful life in Christ.

The work of the kingdom of God is real even when we doubt, but we can be tempted to live as if it isn't real. That's the danger. There's nothing easy about discussing our faith with people who see it as an antiquated fairy tale, and the times to come aren't going to make it any easier. We need to bolster ourselves and encourage one another to trust the truth in the face of others' aggressive unbelief. We need to be aware of the pitfall of viewing our faith through the lenses worn by those who don't know Jesus. Those lenses filter the truth about the living God and cause the viewer to conduct life as if God weren't the significant factor.

We Covet Cows

The second reason we aren't toppling more giants is that, while God gives us everything we need for life and godliness, we still crave something fancy for our faith—like a shiny golden cow, not a handful of boring beans we almost don't trust to work.

This isn't a new problem. While Moses was up on Mount Sinai receiving the commandments from God, the Israelites pooled their gold to create their own god in the form of a calf idol (Exodus 32). They had just witnessed the miracles and power of God enacted on their behalf in their deliverance from Pharaoh, yet they were already weary of following a God no one else could see. They craved a cool, golden idol like the ones all the other nations were worshiping.

We're like them, aren't we? I know I am. We want flash and glitter. Gods with curb appeal. Marketing plans and awesome logos. Flashy numbers and high-definition graphics. Faith with an undeniable cool factor. We have a relentless craving for something new, but what we're ultimately chasing is a worthless cow that won't give milk.

Ever try to milk a golden cow? That ain't happening. A golden cow is for show, not nourishment. In our times, "show" faiths abound, but our God is no song-and-dance man. He's not campaigning for your soul's vote. He isn't interested in upping his "wow factor." God doesn't have to create buzz about himself because he provides beans that contain the promise of life. That's the choice: an inanimate golden cow or the power of life.

Hold a bean—a kidney or lima bean—in the palm of your hand. (I'll wait while you get one.) It appears dry, unappealing, completely lacking in excitement. You know, however, locked within that bean is the power of green, growing life. The power to nourish. The power to satisfy hunger. The power to provide hope. That power isn't apparent on the surface; it's unleashed when we bury the bean.

We grow bored by the tools of our faith because we don't actually put these tools into practice. It's important for Christians not just to believe in God but also to believe God, trust what he says enough to obey him. The enemy has been clever to convince us that what God offers is dry and boring—and it is, if we allow his truth to remain on the surface. But if we bury it deep in the soil of our souls and expose it to the light and the living water of Jesus Christ, we find ourselves clinging to the true Vine, Jesus Christ (John 15). We discover that we, too, are giant-killers.

Designed for New

Our insatiable desire for something new isn't inherently wrong. God designed us for new works, relationships, frontiers, missions, and adventures. He's an imaginative, creative, inventive God with new things to show us every day. We would see more of these if we didn't allow the world and our old sinful natures to misdirect us, tempting us to focus our hunger for *new* away from the development of these long-known qualities, these beans.

The surprise is the result of cultivating the life these "old" beans contain: we're better equipped for new adventures. We appeal to God to show us something new, and he tells us he's provided the pathway for that if we would simply trust him enough to walk it. This is the understanding we gain by studying God's Word; in particular, the passage written in 2 Peter 1:1-10.

The first two verses say this: "Simeon Peter, a servant and apostle of Jesus Christ, To those who have obtained a faith of equal standing with ours by the righteousness of our God and Savior Jesus Christ: May grace and peace be multiplied to you in the knowledge of God and of Jesus our Lord" (ESV).

Such a promising opening! Peter says God calls us into a "faith of equal standing." It's a potent encouragement. Before the cross, the resurrection, and Pentecost, Peter's fear, like a personal Goliath, shouted down his loyalty to his Lord. Afterward, however, Peter joined the ranks of giant-killers, willing even to defy the Pharisees and the powers of Rome.

Prior to encountering Jesus, Peter was a guy like any you'd encounter at the grocery store, the ball field, or the office. He was earthy, gregarious, hardworking, and focused on getting by day to day. Through his relationship with Jesus, Peter became the rock on which Christ built his church with a vision for life that extended into eternity. How inspiring is it that we have obtained a faith of equal standing to Peter's faith?

Knowledge of Christ

The apostle's encouraging words continue in 2 Peter 1:3: "His divine power has granted to us all things that pertain to life and godliness, through the knowledge of him who called us to his own glory and excellence" (ESV).

Knowledge of Christ is key. This is the second time Peter references our knowledge of God and Jesus Christ within the span of three verses. Through our knowledge of Jesus—that comes by salvation, by his Word, by fellowship with other believers, and sometimes by suffering—God grants us all things that pertain to life and godliness. We have everything we need to take on the giants we encounter in this life. This is the truth no matter how we feel. This truth overrides our emotions, the voices in our heads, and our doubts about ourselves compared to others.

Knowing Jesus isn't a onetime event that happens at conversion. Jesus takes an eternity to know. There are probably many people who would say they know you, aren't there? Some know you only by face or by name. Others know you superficially as a coworker, another mom on the playground, or the funny man in their study group. Some, such as your dentist, mechanic, or accountant, know you in specific ways. Others, such as your parents, spouse, or best friend, have a deeper knowledge of you. Peter had a deep knowledge of Jesus, a knowledge forged by walking with him day after day. A knowledge obtained by studying Jesus, obeying Jesus, and suffering in Jesus's name.

Bury the Beans

It isn't enough to acquaint ourselves with Jesus or to learn a few facts about his life. James says even the demons believe Jesus is who he says he is (James 2:19), so knowing that fact isn't enough. Every day we can grow in our knowledge of our Lord. As our knowledge of him expands, so does our ability to access his power for life and godliness in a world that celebrates death and opposes its own Creator.

Peter continues in 2 Peter 1:4: "He has granted to us his precious and very great promises, so that through them you may become partakers of the divine nature, having escaped from the corruption that is in the world because of sinful desire" (ESV).

He has granted us his "precious and very great promises"—like the promise of a seed. You can hold a dry bean in your hand and know that within it is the promise of life waiting to break out. Just as surely, you have within you his power-packed promises waiting to burst forth with new life. If Jack's mother hadn't given those beans the proper conditions to reveal the life they hid inside, it would have remained locked away like an untapped secret. We do this, though, don't we? We store the promises of God on bookshelves or keep them locked inside church buildings, afraid to bring them out and bury them in the mulch of our daily lives. How much more of their potential would we discover if we did?

I don't know about you, but I need to pause and catch my breath, especially because in the next part of 2 Peter 1, he spills the beans holding the key to our effectiveness as believers. I need a moment to process. I'll catch up with you in chapter 4.

Small Steps Toward Slaying Giants

1. Read Exodus 32. God had just delivered the Israelites from Egypt shortly before they created the golden calf. What does this tell you about our susceptibility to worship idols? What are some "golden cows" people are tempted to worship in your culture, in your community?
2. Many of us relate to Peter. In Matthew 16:13-23, we glimpse Peter impressing Jesus with his understanding of who Jesus is, followed immediately by Jesus scolding Peter for setting his mind on the things of man, not God! Can you relate to the Israelites and to Peter in the ups and downs of your spiritual life? What hope does it give you that Jesus used Peter in such a powerful way in the work of building the kingdom of God?
3. List the people, places, or influences affecting the way you view your relationship with Jesus. Which of them encourage you to see your faith as God sees it? Which of them tempt you to see your faith the way Jack's mother viewed the magic beans?
4. Prayerfully consider three steps that you can take to defend against a worthless-beans view of your life with Christ. Do you need to increase your knowledge of Jesus? Do you need more prayer support when engaging with certain individuals or activities? Do you need to spend more time with people who encourage you to have a godly view of faith?

One Stone for Your Sling: God doesn't have to create buzz about himself because he provides beans that contain the promise of life. That's the choice: an inanimate golden cow or the power of life.

4

Where Peter Spills the Beans

Beans that remain unburied keep their secrets locked away. The trouble for most of us, though, is that gardening looks a lot like work.

Some of us will find ourselves challenged by the next half of Peter's passage because it involves a word we don't hear often in today's discussions of faith. That word is *effort*. That's right. We're going to talk about putting effort into our faith. Other translations use the word *diligence,* defined as persistent work or effort. When I first encountered 2 Peter 1:5, "For this very reason, make every effort to supplement your faith" (ESV), I had to pause to consider what it would mean to put effort into spiritual growth.

Grace Is Foundational

God's grace is foundational to my faith. Since childhood, I've known the truth. I can do nothing to earn the salvation provided for me in Jesus Christ. I believe this completely. We're saved by grace, and nothing we do adds to the work of Jesus Christ. Peter isn't teaching anything contrary to grace in this passage.

I also pause because, like others, I tend toward overachievement and a self-centered pursuit of perfection. This makes it easy for me to fall into the trap (the lie) of believing I have to be good to earn God's favor. Frequently I strive when I should rest. At times I trust my efforts when I should rely on the power of the Holy Spirit.

When I read a passage of Scripture that talks about "making every effort," I stop to remind myself of the following truths so as not to fall prey to trying to earn God's pleasure. If you are like me, you will appreciate my pausing here to remind us all what Jesus has done for us.

There's no effort on our part that earns our way into heaven or into relationship with our heavenly Father. Our salvation is a gift of grace through Jesus Christ alone (Ephesians 2:1-10). Paul devotes much of the books of Romans, Galatians, and Ephesians to teaching that we're saved by grace alone, not by works. When my heavenly Father sees me, he sees me through the sacrifice of his Son, Jesus, and I rest in his favor. If you have entered into a saving relationship with Jesus Christ, you, too, freely receive his grace.

Easy Is Not Guaranteed

Let me also remind us that having God's favor is no guarantee of an easy life, prayers answered just the way we'd like, and every dream fulfilled the way we envision. We find in the biblical record that God's people suffered as much as, if not more than, those around them did. Matthew 5:45 says, "He makes the sun rise on both the evil and the good and sends rain on both the righteous and the unrighteous."

None of us will achieve perfection this side of glory. Fortunately, God doesn't base his pleasure on our perfection but wholly on Jesus Christ. Peter isn't writing a prescription here for answered prayers or for earning God's favor. He teaches the value of developing these qualities, but it isn't about making God happy or attaining more stuff from God. Jesus already obtained God's pleasure for us. Our lives this side of glory aren't about getting everything we want.

That said, modern believers are so conscious of promoting salvation by grace alone that sometimes we discourage effort of any kind in the Christian life. We're sensitive (as we should be) to Christians who've been hurt by legalism or false teaching, and so, understandably, we devote significant time to the truth that forgiveness is ours through Christ alone. Neglecting to talk about passages like 2 Peter 1:1-10, however, can lead to a dangerous overcorrection resulting in sloppy, lazy, ineffective spiritual lives. Then we wonder why we're not equipped to survive in a land of giants.

Make Every Effort

Peter doesn't simply tell us to try; he instructs us to "make every effort to supplement [our] faith." I don't know what that sounds like to you, but to me it sounds like hard work. That's daunting because I have the tendency to lean in the other direction. No one would call me lazy (well, not to my face), but sometimes I like to skip a step or two. I'm a "close enough" kind of girl. Allow me to illustrate.

I'd love to say I always put every effort into my housekeeping. I'd love to say it, but I'd be lying. There are times I, you know, skimp. For instance, there was the time when my children were young and I forgot to switch the washing machine from small-load capacity to large before I washed a big load of clothes. I noticed it once the machine stopped but decided it wasn't worth the effort to redo. What would be the harm?

The next day, my son went for a run on the bike path. It was a drizzly day, so I remained in my car reading a book. After a few minutes, I glanced up and noticed white flecks on the knees of Zack's running gear. After another turn, he jogged over and knocked on my window. "Mom, what's going on with my pants? My knees are foaming!"

It took me a moment to realize those sweats had been in the load I'd short-changed for water. There hadn't been enough to rinse them clean of soap, so now Zack's running and the drizzle had agitated them to a good white lather. His legs were red and irritated, and he was running through town with foamy knees because I'd given the task less effort than it had deserved.[1]

I'm not talking about housework here, though, and neither was Peter. I mean to encourage you (and me) to make every effort in our faith, our spiritual growth. To approach our faith with diligence. To endeavor consistently, rigorously, and carefully to grow up in Jesus Christ.

When a Jewish scribe asked Jesus what the greatest commandment was, this was his reply: "You must love the Lord your God with all your heart, with all your being, with all your mind, and with all your strength" (Mark 12:30). Modern believers have a great appreciation for applying all our hearts, all our beings (souls), and all our minds, but we're baffled when we reach the exhortation to love the Lord with all our strength. We're confused because we're out of practice applying strength. It makes more sense that all our strength comes into play when we understand that our faith requires effort applied daily.

The Boring Beans

I encourage you to pay attention to Peter's words and practice what he says next in 2 Peter 1:5-7: "For this very reason, make every effort to supplement your faith with virtue, and virtue with knowledge, and knowledge with self-control, and self-control with steadfastness, and steadfastness with godliness, and godliness with brotherly affection, and brotherly affection with love" (ESV).

Here is where Peter spills the beans. There's no flashy packaging in this passage. Peter packs it with content and trusts the beans to sell themselves. Too often we start reading this list and our minds slip into a lower gear. To many, especially those who are not in relationship with Jesus, these characteristics appear as boring as a handful of dry beans.

Blah, blah, blah! we think. Faith. Virtue. Knowledge. Self-control. Steadfastness. Godliness. Brotherly affection. Love. We might justifiably refer to them as the eight boring beans of the Christian faith. In these modern times, one can be hard-pressed to recognize their worth.

Cows seem much cooler—especially golden cows. Other popular spiritual disciplines with their enthusiasts and gurus offer flashier menus on the path to spiritual growth. These might include cleansings, postures, mountain treks, rituals, fire-walks, special diets, and spiritual audits. Other worldviews boast shiny golden cows of options intended to make us spiritually cool and help us achieve enlightenment.

There's nothing wrong with climbing mountains, facing our fears, or increasing insight into our lives, but other worldviews promote a pathway to peace that excludes Jesus. They dismiss the qualities Peter encourages us to make every effort to obtain. In contrast to the shiny new cows of the world, Peter's promoting stuff that true God-followers have promoted for centuries—faith, virtue, knowledge, self-control, steadfastness, godliness, brotherly affection, and love. Old-fashioned. Archaic. Outdated. Snooze fest! You can almost see the dust fly around these qualities.

What modern person wants to put effort into obtaining virtue? Imagine trying to engage a new generation by promoting self-control. Love? Don't get me started. Seriously, don't we already know everything there is to know about love? When a minister says the topic of the morning's sermon is love, three-quarters of us tune out as if we're watching a rerun of *Gilligan's Island.* (We'd likely pay more attention to Gilligan!)

Why Invest in Ancient Virtues?

When faced with a list of spiritual golden oldies like this, it's natural to ask some probing questions: What's our motivation for working to supplement our faith with these qualities? Where's the payoff? Why invest in ancient virtues and qualities that today's society discounts or dismisses outright? Why shouldn't we toss this handful of boring beans right out the window and run back to see if there's a chance we can still retrieve our cow?

These are the whispers of the enemy, loved one. It's a brilliantly wicked weapon to convince us the very tools of life, the qualities God promises will bear fruit in our lives, are boring and useless. The evil one is crafty. We mustn't fall prey to his deception, but for a long time we have.

Fortunately, Peter understands us. Remember, Peter is an ordinary man who entered a relationship with Jesus. He's like us, subject to the same foibles and failings, and yet he testifies to what happens when a regular person gives everything he has to Jesus. He also hears the question we're asking: what's in it for us to work at developing these qualities in our lives?

Effective, Fruitful Spiritual Lives

Peter explains the power of these qualities in 2 Peter 1:8: "For if these qualities are yours and are increasing, they keep you from being ineffective or unfruitful in the knowledge of our Lord Jesus Christ" (ESV).

Don't miss the impact of this tiny verse. Inhale the fresh air of these twenty-five words. There's power here. Power for unleashing the life inside a boring bean. These qualities in increasing measure make us giant-killers!

Do you ever feel ineffective as a Christian? Do you ever feel unfruitful spiritually? Pay attention. These are no ordinary beans. These aren't boring disciplines relegated to antiquity. This is no eight-step self-improvement program. Oh no, this is about more than becoming better citizens. Bury these beans in the dirt of your life, the soil of your soul, and prepare to discover your giant-killing potential.

Remember Peter was writing at a time when the church faced giants similar to the ones we face today. Persecution from without. False teaching and immaturity from within. The world in turmoil and the early church asking the same questions we are. How do we survive these times? How do we best minister to those around us? How do we determine which teachers expound the truth and which are off track? If we know and love Jesus, why do we feel so small and ineffective in the times in which we live? Peter explains if we have these qualities in increasing measure, we'll be effective and fruitful in our faith.

Then, for emphasis, Peter explains what happens if we neglect these qualities in 2 Peter 1:9-10: "For whoever lacks these qualities is so nearsighted that he is blind, having forgotten that he was cleansed from his former sins. Therefore, brothers, be all the more diligent to confirm your calling and election, for if you practice these qualities you will never fall" (ESV).

Do we want to avoid spiritual blindness? Yes. Do we want to remember we are free from sin? Of course. Do we want to walk with Christ in such a way that we will never fall? A resounding yes from me, and I'm sure also from you. Then we need to be asking Jesus to develop within us these powerful qualities.

It's challenging. Let's remind ourselves of that from the start. It requires an investment of time, strength, energy, and heart. A renewing of our minds. Reading this list is not the same as knowing what these qualities look like played out in real life. We need to become students of these qualities. Ask God to develop them in us. Research every passage of Scripture that teaches about them, and put into practice what those passages say. We'll need to find examples of these qualities in Scripture and in one another so we develop a bank of role models. (There's help for this process in Part 3.)

Making the Climb

There is no graduated program to developing these qualities. Developing them in increasing measure is much like climbing a beanstalk. We can point one another in the right direction and offer advice on upcoming handholds, but really, each of us has to make our way up the vine with the strength and power of the Lord. We need to put in every effort.

When I was a young adult, I wanted to impress an eligible man in my church, so I volunteered to help him lead the teens on a rappelling trip. Never mind that I had never done any rock climbing. Never mind that I had the upper-arm strength of a jellyfish. I focused not on what the trip might require but on attracting his attention.

Bravely (foolishly), I volunteered to be the first to rappel the cliff. I felt secure enough in the belay, and, after summoning the courage to take the first step, I enjoyed the descent. I felt confident and hopeful this would be the start of a beautiful relationship... until I reached the bottom and learned the only way back was straight up the rock face I'd just come down. An endeavor for which I was not equipped.

I'm embarrassed to say the ascent took me the rest of the morning. Every other climber scrambled up and down the wall several times as I, with constant encouragement and the patience of two teens taking turns climbing beside me to identify handholds, scaled the cliff, weeping the whole way. There was no shortcut or work-around. No one could do it for me (although I'm sure they wish they could have). There was no fast forward. I impressed no one, but I've never forgotten that climb.

Spiritual growth is like that wall. Others can teach us, guide us, and encourage us, but we spend our own strength on the ascent.

We Are Giant-Killers

Likewise, each of us must invest the effort in developing these qualities. Peter assures us that if we do, we'll find ourselves effective and fruitful in the Christian life. What better outcome can we hope for than that? Too many of us believe the lie that the key to our lives is doing more. Some of us have come to believe the key is doing less. Really, the key isn't what we do; it's who we are, in increasing measure. Fortunately, in Christ, we are giant-killers.

Remember, we're people who live in a land of giants. We're small, but God loves working with the small. And, through Jesus, we come from a long line of giant-killers. If we refuse to see ourselves through the world's eyes but, instead, see the promise of life within us and the power of putting into practice what God teaches in his Word, and if we trust that the beans we received when we traded our cows really do contain power and life, then we will be effective at toppling giants.

How do we trade in our cows and bury these beans in our lives? Thoughts on that and practical steps are in Part 2.

Small Steps Toward Slaying Giants

1. Read the list of eight qualities (page 28) and write your gut reaction to developing them in your life. Do you feel hopeful? Discouraged? Doubtful? Eager? What's your previous experience with working to develop these qualities? Where have you seen success, and where have you been frustrated? Confess any fears or hesitations about investing effort in these qualities and ask God to help you see the process through his eyes.
2. It's good to remind ourselves regularly that our salvation is a gift of grace through Jesus Christ alone. Our efforts are not about earning our way to eternity but about increasing our effectiveness this side of glory. Read these passages on grace and thank God for Jesus Christ: Romans 3:21-28; 5:1-11, 8; Ephesians 2:1-10; Galatians 2:15-21.
3. Think about how children or plants grow and change. A child isn't born able to walk. We make numerous attempts and fall down a lot before mastering the art of walking upright. In the same way, flowers don't emerge from the soil in full bloom. They spend time hidden in the earth and erupt from the soil requiring tending or certain conditions to reach their potential. Why do we think spiritual growth is any different? Why do we imagine that overnight we can decide to be loving, virtuous, or godly without some falls or some cultivating? Find a drawing or photo of a favorite plant or of yourself as a child to serve as a reminder that God sees us all in process.
4. Consider what support will help as you study this passage and seek God's guidance in making every effort to increase in these qualities. Do you work best within a small group? With a mentor? With an accountability partner? Alone with a journal? Ask God to direct you to the best helps to encourage spiritual growth.
5. Think about what Jesus means to you. Look again at the list of giants in your life and in our world. What would it mean to you to become

fruitful and effective in the knowledge of our Lord Jesus Christ? Write this down to refer to as you take the next steps in this process of spiritual growth.

❧ ❧ ❧

One Stone for Your Sling: "For if these qualities are yours and are increasing, they keep you from being ineffective or unfruitful in the knowledge of our Lord Jesus Christ" (2 Peter 1:8 ESV).

PART 2

Trading in Our Cows

A hardworking farmer should get the first share of the crop. Think about what I'm saying; the Lord will give you understanding about everything.

2 Timothy 2:6-7

Part 2 teaches strategic thinking about cultivating attitudes and expectations leading to spiritual growth in a culture opposed to Christ, and it presents an approach to culture that can improve our effectiveness in outreach and ministry.

5

Loving Jack's Mom

Some days it's hard not to side with Jack's mother, isn't it?

If my family were hungry and someone handed me seeds, I'd be hard-pressed to display gratitude. When my family is hungry today, I don't want a solution for tomorrow—especially one that might not reap a harvest for over a hundred tomorrows!

Years ago while working in a fitness center, I lost over twenty pounds. I enjoyed the loose fit of my sweat pants until I had an unfortunate encounter with a recumbent bike. I was rushing (needlessly) through the gym when I lazily navigated a shortcut to the paper towel dispenser by squeezing between two members pedaling away. The pocket of my oversized sweats caught on the side-adjustment handle of one of the bikes. When I moved forward, my pants slipped halfway down my thighs.

That's right. Workout and a floor show, compliments of my haste! Fortunately, my pants hiked up as quickly as they came down. I retreated to my office until the memory of my Hanes faded from everyone's memory.

You'd think by my age, I would have learned my lesson about shortcuts. I had to literally get caught with my pants down to commit to reformation. In the workout world, everyone wants a shortcut. It's no different in the world of modern spiritual growth. God, though, is an advocate for taking the long way, and he's right.

A Countercultural Pace

Christians have always had to navigate the tension inherent in experiencing the needs of the present while investing in eternal rewards. We romanticize the past, but truly, it's never been easy to walk the long, narrow path and avoid tempting detours or promising shortcuts. Today, though, the challenge has taken on epic proportions.

In modern culture, people who score big money, great success, or substantial numbers rate titanic attention. Readers made billionaire Donald Trump's book *The Art of the Deal* a number-one best seller. Moviegoers demand endless photos of the latest Hollywood "It Girl." Sports fans herald pro athletes, not only for their skills but also for the brands they build, capitalizing on their talents and their names—especially when their fortunate rises are meteoric.

That's the new facet to the achievement diamond in our times: fast money, swift success. Rags-to-riches stories have always been popular, but to garner our attention now, they must include an element of acceleration. Modern audiences value high yield with rapid turnaround. In an age of drive-thru and express lanes, no one's interested in observing speed limits or taking the scenic route to results. We no longer respect people who pay their dues; instead we consider them pedestrian, dupes, or lacking in ambition or brains. We herald those who skip *Go* and still collect their two hundred dollars, as if life were a game of Monopoly for the swift and clever.

Welcome to the challenge of spiritual growth in the twenty-first century. We elevate ministries that accomplish impressive numbers quickly. We follow the ones drawing crowds, gaining followers for Jesus by the thousands. We seek to maximize the effectiveness of our message to the most people in the fastest way. We challenge ourselves to think bigger and faster and to employ optimal graphics. If we have a message to get out, why shouldn't we want to deliver it globally?

There's a place for this thinking. God calls some to impact crowds and colossal audiences. Everything has its season. On the day of Pentecost, Peter addressed those gathered in Jerusalem, and the church grew by three thousand souls in one day (Acts 2:41). It isn't unusual when God moves into a new region, country, or people group to hear stories of mass conversions. We can't look down on brothers and sisters with visions to reach out for Christ in big ways.

Raising God's Children

But effective follow-up from these Christian baby booms includes a plan for growth. That requires a long-term, slow-yield mind-set. Just as it's easier to conceive and give birth to babies than to raise them, the process of disciple making doesn't end on the day of conversion. It's challenging to encourage believers to grow up in Christ, particularly when they value fast results and associate maturity with loss of innovation, vitality, and creativity. When a society worships Peter Pan, people don't easily catch a vision for maturation. In the world where leading phone apps start with "Insta" and "Snap," it's going to be work to convince people of the value of long-term growth over time. Nothing, however—even encouraging baby believers to grow up in the twenty-first century—is impossible with God.

Grown-Up Babies

Another challenge for spiritual growth is finding a way to discuss it without engaging in comparisons. It helps to remember the church is a family. Parents don't favor one child because he's older or consider younger children lesser because they don't yet ride bikes. Families assign tasks appropriately, considering each child's age, gifts, and maturity. We don't ask three-year-olds to cook breakfast, but they can feed the chickens. Likewise, we expect most fifteen-year-olds to oversee their younger siblings for an evening, but we hope they're past needing a chore chart.

Immaturity in toddlers isn't a problem; it's appropriate and to be expected. If a child continues to throw tantrums or require bottle-feeding into grade school, however, we recognize it as a developmental issue needing immediate intervention. I'm not sure why we've lost that perspective in the church, but too often, we tolerate long-term believers behaving like babies. We rush immature believers into leadership roles too quickly or demand so much from mature believers that we exhaust them into early ministry retirement.

One of Paul's favorite themes to the church is the need to grow up. The writer of Hebrews also favors the topic, summing it up neatly and frankly in Hebrews 6:1-8:

> So let's press on to maturity, by moving on from the basics about Christ's word. Let's not lay a foundation of turning away from dead works, of faith in God, of teaching about ritual ways to wash with water, laying on of hands, the resurrection from the dead, and eternal judgment—all over again. We're going to press on, if God allows it.
>
> Because it's impossible to restore people to changed hearts and lives who turn away once they have seen the light, tasted the heavenly gift, become partners with the Holy Spirit, and tasted God's good word and the powers of the coming age. They are crucifying God's Son all over again and exposing him to public shame. The ground receives a blessing from God when it drinks up the rain that regularly comes and falls on it and yields a useful crop for those people for whom it is being farmed. But if it produces thorns and thistles, it's useless and close to being cursed. It ends up being burned.

The writer concludes with a farming reference because the attitude of a farmer is another one that serves us well when discussing spiritual growth.

A Farmer's View

In 2 Timothy 2:1-7, Paul likens the Christian life to one of a soldier, an athlete, and a farmer. Soldiers sacrifice and keep themselves alert because they're engaged in battle. Likewise, believers play their part in the spiritual war for souls. Athletes train hard and exercise discipline in order to run their races well, and so we do well to train in our faith. Farmers exhibit quiet, diligent, consistent, patient attendance to their fields. They sow the seeds in good soil. They water, weed, and wait, knowing ultimately that God is the one who calls forth life from the earth. Farmers respect the work, but they're deeply aware that they labor in tandem with God.

This is the perfect lens from which to view the passage from Peter. He says if we have the eight qualities in increasing measure, we will be effective and fruitful in our knowledge of Jesus Christ. Developing these characteristics, then, isn't something we achieve like winning a battle or completing a race. It's akin to the growth of a living being, a continuous, though not always visual, process.

When I was forty, God allowed me to lead a Bible study for a group of women with black belts in karate. They wanted to study God's Word weekly after class. This meant, they explained, I would need to take karate. If you've ever wondered if God has a sense of humor, let me assure you, he does. Why else place a nonathletic, overweight, middle-aged, uncoordinated woman in a white uniform, compel her to stand in front of a mirror surrounded by fit, fighting, unchurched martial artists, and ask her to teach the Bible? During my first week, I was so intimidated I could barely stand, never mind learn to block and punch. But I learned a pivotal spiritual lesson early on.

The adult karate students started each class together, arranged by rank, to practice their basic moves as one. Although I was new to martial arts, the basic blocks and punches weren't complicated so I followed along with the higher-ranked students. The karate teacher, or sensei—a fifth-degree black belt—moved among us, praising or correcting our execution. I was shocked when he paused to correct third- and fourth-degree black belts in the front row.

How, I wondered, is it possible that they still need correction on basics I learned in one week? Was it a failing of the karate school or of the individuals? I learned it was neither. Martial arts students embrace a mind-set of continual, perpetual improvement. No one ever truly masters a move, but once a student learns it, he or she commits to a lifetime of perfecting it. That lesson was humbling and inspiring at once.

How is it that karate students understand this concept but the modern church still struggles to adopt its wisdom? I thought God sent me to the unchurched at the dojo to teach, but he showed me then that it would be a reciprocal relationship from beginning to end.

Soul-Deep Transformation

While it isn't hard to get people to look like mature Christians quickly, genuine spiritual growth can be an agonizingly slow process. For centuries, society promoted the kind of social conditioning and pressure required to get large numbers of people to conform to the appearance of Christianity. It looked as though entire nations accepted the truth of Christ, the authority of God's Word, and scriptural truth. Unfortunately, countless individuals simply learned to hide their sins beneath religious camouflage. When this hard truth surfaced, many fell away, disenchanted.

The time for expecting people to behave like Christians without knowing Christ has passed. Perhaps it served a purpose, and God brought good from it, but eventually it resulted in extensive disillusionment with the church. We're drowning in the aftermath from the mass exodus of young people burnt by hypocrisy to the tearing down of anything traditional that smacks of those old days. Society is tossing out many good babies with that hypocritical bathwater.

God transforms us, not through our willful self-restraint but by the process of spiritual growth brought about by relationship with Jesus, obedience, and Spirit-powered effort. For those of us who strive, the pitfalls of approaching this passage are either to ignore it because the endeavor seems like a tiring venture or to attack the process as if every ounce of growth depended on our own strength. If you've ever tried to yank at a plant to get it to grow or if you've ever willed a child to move on to his or her next stage, you'll appreciate the futility of that kind of effort in the pursuit of healthy spiritual growth. Farmers know that even with their best work, they're still dependent on God for their crops.

My little girl always moved at her own pace, and it was seldom fast enough for me. One day as I tried to get everyone out the door, I stood by as she methodically donned her socks and shoes. I thought I was exhibiting Herculean self-restraint until she looked up and said, "Mom, I need you to be patient."

I responded, "I am being patient."

To which she replied, "No, you're just looking patient. It's not the same thing."

Nailed by a preschooler.

It's not enough for Christians to *appear* to have faith, virtue, knowledge, self-control, steadfastness, godliness, brotherly affection, and love. Our call is not to *appear* to be like Christ; it is to *be* like Christ. This happens only through a willing partnership with God.

From Jack's mom's perspective it's an impossibility, but we have God's perspective. As challenging as it is to pursue spiritual maturity in a Peter Pan world, God equips us for the times in which we live. We know Jack's mom and we accept her, but we love her enough to want her to move beyond the longing for her lost cow. We want her to see what happens when she unlocks the power of the beans. Moreover, we can't keep this to ourselves because, as we'll discover in the next chapter, you and I know the place to find food in a famished society. It's a secret we must share.

Small Steps Toward Slaying Giants

1. Consider the pitfalls and challenges of promoting spiritual growth. Where do we get our models for growth? How can meditating on the growth of children to adulthood or seeds to harvest help us develop a healthy perspective on the spiritual growth of believers?
2. What are ways we promote growth in children? How can we translate that to promoting growth in the church? What are ways we intervene when a child's growth has stalled or been thwarted in some way? How can this understanding inform our interactions within the body of Christ?
3. Plants and people sometimes encounter conditions that interrupt their growth process. Improper nourishment, lack of water, bad storms, abuse, lazy parenting, and disease are things that can contribute to poor growth. We don't blame the child or the plant for not thriving when these conditions occur, but we do take steps to address and correct what we can so growth can continue. What situations or conditions have interfered with growth in your life or in the life of your church? What's one step you could take to address them and move forward?
4. What does Ephesians 4:11-16 say about God's expectation of spiritual growth? What has God given us to facilitate spiritual growth? What kind of teamwork is involved in encouraging spiritual growth within the church?

One Stone for Your Sling: Our call is not to *appear* to be like Christ; it is to *be* like Christ. This happens only through a willing partnership with God.

6

Surviving the Famine

God's enemies aren't inventive, but most of the time, they don't need to be. We keep falling for the same old tricks, don't we?

The vicious and persistent attack on the authority of Scripture in our times is nothing new. Genesis 3:1 records that the serpent's first approach with Eve was to cast doubt on God's Word: "The snake was the most intelligent of all the wild animals that the LORD God had made. He said to the woman, 'Did God really say that you shouldn't eat from any tree in the garden?' "

Did God really say . . . ? That is the insidious wedge of doubt employed from the dawn of time to now. Evil has no need to invent a new strategy because many in each generation fall for this one. The forces of darkness understand the power of God's Word, so their initial assault on anyone with access to God's Word is to tempt him or her to doubt it, fear it, or disbelieve it altogether.

When my son was a boy, he loved video games. We allowed them but applied time limits and rules. Wandering through a game store one day, I heard him translate my gaming guidelines to one of his friends: "We're Christians so we have rules about what games I can play: no games with naked or half-naked people, and we can only kill people if there's a good reason." That was his interpretation of our prohibiting games rated for mature audiences and allowing a World War II–based strategy game but not games where he might shoot people for sport. I think back to that conversation when I'm about to translate God's laws for others. I imagine I sound, to my heavenly Father, as Zack sounded to me.

Famished for God's Word

In 2014, the Barna Group, an evangelical Christian polling firm, "For the first time since tracking began, Bible skepticism is tied with Bible engagement."[1] The report showed that out of those surveyed, 19 percent identified as Bible skeptics (responding with the most negative or nonsacred view of the Bible) and 19 percent as Bible-engaged (read the Bible at least four times a week and believe it is the Word of God). Now consider alongside those statistics this one. According to BBC News, one of the requirements for the United Nations to declare a famine is "at least 20% of the population has access to fewer than 2,100 kilocalories of food a day."[2] These are fascinating statistics to consider side-by-side because the Old Testament prophets warned of a time to come when there would be a famine for the Word of the Lord (Amos 8:11).

Are we there yet? I don't know. As I write this, God's Word is still readily available to us in the West, but if the statistics are true, many of us have entered a time of voluntary famine by not availing ourselves of it or by deciding it's of little or no worth. Famines occur, not only because of food scarcity but also because circumstances of war cut off food supply. Spiritual warfare could probably, then, play a contributing role in a famine of the Word of the Lord.

This isn't a book about prophecy, but there is value in understanding the times. There was a period when at least American and European Christians lived and ministered in cultures in which even many unsaved had a working knowledge of and respect for God's Word. The Bible was studied in public schools and considered something with which educated people were familiar. The Ten Commandments were posted in courthouses, and business closed on Sundays. Classic writers popular with the masses, such as Dickens or Steinbeck, could make literary biblical references and assume readers would make the connection. We've clearly entered a time when that won't be true. Whether or not it's the prophesied famine, Barna's statistic means that close to one in five people will, like Jack's mom, have little or no biblical context from which to understand our worldview.

The Barna poll further reveals only about one in five of us engages with

God's Word at least four times a week. That's the statistic for those of us who, in Jack-like fashion, believe it is God's Word! That leaves three out of five of us floundering somewhere in the middle, dangerously at risk of being sucked into the swirling drain of those who reject or neglect God's Word altogether.

Battling Cultural Drift

If you've spent any time swimming in the ocean, you know how easy it is to drift down the beach with the pull of the tide. When my mom would take my brother and me swimming in the Atlantic, she'd set up her blanket beside a lifeguard station. Before she'd permit us to swim, we had to agree to line ourselves up with that station every time we rode a wave into shore. Occasionally I forgot the value of that and simply bodysurfed for a few minutes only to emerge in a panic, thinking my mother had moved away. After a time, I'd locate her right in front of the same lifeguard station and shiver at how easily the ocean had taken me far off course without my realizing.

The Bible is like a lifeguard station. God has told us we'll find him when we look for him in his Word and as we follow his Word made flesh, Jesus Christ. Daily we enter the surf of our lives. The prevailing tides naturally tug our souls away from our Father. If we continually realign ourselves with his Word, we'll keep him in view and reduce the risk of losing our way or drifting into danger.

Our first course of action, then, in times when others are starving for the Word of God, is to be sure we receive the proper nourishment for our souls. This is no selfish act of hoarding, because there's plenty, in Christ, for all. This is simply the most effective order in which to accomplish the building of God's kingdom. Just as they warn us on airplanes to secure our own oxygen masks before helping others, so we need to inhale the pure air of truth as taught in the Bible. By doing so, we reduce the risk of being led astray by the noxious gas of deception before we attempt to lead others.

Circling the Wagons

Reading about God's Word is not the same as actually reading his Word. I hesitated to write a book like this for fear readers with many demands on their time would focus more on my words than on God's Word. I've prayed over this book (and asked my prayer team to do the same) that it would incite all who read it to multiply their time in his Word, not distract from it. Spending time with Jesus, the Word made flesh, and reading, studying, meditating on, and memorizing God's Word are pursuits that nourish our souls in a famished land.

We also need to circle the wagons, so to speak, around our faith that God's Word is reliable and true. This is where dark forces make their continuous assault. During World War II, there were enemy radio broadcasters whose sole purpose was to demoralize the troops. Their chief tactic was to cast doubt on the information the soldiers received from their commanders and from home.[3] Our spiritual enemy utilizes a similar tactic.

Know that it's common to have doubts or questions when you're subjected to endless speculations that God's Word is faulted. It can be frightening to read an article, hear a convincing argument, or watch a television show that causes us to doubt the Bible is God's Word, but it's more frightening when we try to face it alone. We don't want to admit to another person we're shaken up, but that's usually the best remedy.

I'm not a theologian or a pastor; I'm an everyday believer. Even though I've read and believed the Bible since childhood, have a degree in biblical studies, and have experienced the power of God's Word, I encounter the assaults. I need reassurance when I'm tempted to falter on this subject.

When I face doubt, I turn to my church leaders, to other mature, believing friends, and to a few reliable books on Christian apologetics. They remind me of the truth and reacquaint me with the evidence (and there is plenty) that "every Scripture is inspired by God and is useful for teaching, for showing mistakes, for correcting, and for training character, so that the person who belongs to God can be equipped to do everything that is good" (2 Timothy 3:16-17). Ask your pastor or one of your church leaders to recommend a book or website considered helpful when facing doubts about the reliability of God's Word. If you hear an argument you can't counter on your own, let someone know. It's better than letting a doubt fester and risk its isolating you from other believers.

The Opposite of Fear

This isn't a scare chapter. In fact, my goal is the opposite of fear. I pray nothing I write incites people to fear, because God commands us not to be afraid. This chapter is an invitation to release fear by allowing love to inform our understanding of these times and the people with whom we share them.

As Christians, we hunger and thirst for righteousness but aren't afraid of this hunger even in a famine because (a) we know what it is and (b) we know the source of spiritual food and avail ourselves of it. But we live surrounded by starving spirits, people with gnawing pits in the bellies of their souls, but no idea what they need. It's important, when ministering or reaching out, to love them and understand their perspective.

These people do have reason to fear and often let that fear drive them. Some have found ways to address their hunger with the equivalent of spiritual junk food. Others have taken to eating what isn't food—counterfeit nourishment—to quiet their souls. Still others have been hungry for so long that their minds are either dulled and apathetic or ravenous and angry. They languish or they lash out. Starvation drives some, like Jack's mom, to such desperation that they make hasty choices they immediately regret. They don't think beyond today.

We Are Here

This also isn't about establishing blame or condemning Barna's 19 percent. This is simply a giant red X on our society's spiritual mall map. We are *here,* on the verge of spiritual famine. Not only are we here, but we also need to keep in mind there are malicious forces at work. They obscure the sign for God's "whole foods store" and try to convince everyone the only nourishment is at the "junk food court." We're the ones who, by God's mercy and grace, know the truth and understand what's happening. We know the power and potential hidden in the beans.

Because of this, we need to be identifiable as well-nourished souls. The well-fed stand out in a starving land. They hardly need to solicit followers, as it's clear they know the way to stores of food.

Christians nourished by God's Word will inspire some to dine beside them. Those who have invested in counterfeit food or who have developed strange appetites they can no longer appease with godly things will be inspired to despise us and will seek our destruction. Still others will have given up on finding what their souls need. They neither follow us nor attack us but instead wait for someone to spoon-feed them. This is the cultural landscape we navigate by faith.

Nothing to Fear

We can use this matrix to fuel our love for others. Secure in our relationship with Jesus and nourished by God's Word, we have nothing to fear. By growing in Christ, we become hallmarks of life in a time of starved souls and as such will inspire others simply by living in their presence. Some will need our compassion as we nurse them to health on the pure milk of biblical basics. Others will despise us, but we trust God either to protect us or to call us to suffer in his name. Either way, we've no reason to fear.

My children were never afraid when they were with their father or with me, not because they didn't understand there were dangers in the world but because they trusted us to care for them. We acknowledge the dangers of living in a famished world deceived by the evil one, but we do not fear because our Father is with us.

How will we find the courage to climb the vine that grows from these beans? I believe Jack will lead the way; but first, let's catch our breath.

Small Steps Toward Slaying Giants

1. Do a Bible word search on *hunger* and *famine*. God has much to say about hunger, and often he relates it to hunger of the soul. What does God say will satisfy soul-hunger in John 6:35? What is the secret of facing hunger revealed in Philippians 4:11-13?
2. Where would you fall on the Barna survey? What step will you take to improve either your understanding of God's Word or your commitment to spending time reading it? Make a plan to take that step today.
3. Listen to Michael Card's song "So Many Books" (find it online or at a local Christian bookstore). Brainstorm with a friend or small group things you can do to improve other people's access to God's Word. Can you pray for people still waiting to receive his Word in their language? Are there resources you can contribute toward translation work? What about locally—how are you using your gifts to expose others to God's Word or to help others understand it? What creative approaches can you devise to get God's Word in front of people in your community? Implement one of your ideas.
4. Read Psalm 37 every day this week and write verses of particular comfort on sticky notes or index cards to have available when anxious thoughts appear.

One Stone for Your Sling: The well-fed stand out in a starving land.

7

Jack Was Nothing Without the Vine

The beanstalk is really the story's main character. Jack was nothing without the vine.

One of my favorite memories is of my daughter, seven or eight years old, running along the Atlantic shore, shouting, "This is what I was made for, Mom! I was made to run on the beach and jump in the waves!" It certainly felt like it at that moment. She was joyous, covered with sand, and dancing in the saltwater. It was one of my happiest life moments, enjoying her revel.

My son, Zack, had a moment of joy like that, but it came after considerable struggle. At an age far beyond when other kids had abandoned their training wheels, I'd driven him to an old airstrip to push the issue. His father removed the metal wheel stabilizers from his two-wheeler, and we spent the good part of an hour with my holding the bars and his gathering courage to balance without support. Exasperated, I insisted he try it once without help.

He argued that I seemed to want him to fall. "What kind of mother doesn't care if her kid might get hurt?" he hollered. "Fine. I'll go get hurt!" With that, he shoved off to spite me. To our surprise, he took off. Finally he rode his bike. Rounding a curve on the asphalt track, he called out, "Mom! I'm doing it! Look at me. I'm really doing it!" The memory still makes me smile.

God designed us to know him and enjoy him forever, to experience the kind of joy and purpose my daughter knew at the seaside. It's easy to lose sight of the enjoyment part. Many of us have barely grazed the surface of our capacity for God adventures, and that's because, much like my son and his training wheels, we cling to the comfort of the basic teachings of our faith, fearing the inevitable scrapes and bruises inherent in venturing out toward deeper growth.

We need to hold to these basic teachings but also grow in them and expand our use of them in serving God and others. People who've known Jesus for years should be far different from who they were when they first met him, not continuing to wrestle with their former sins or trying to grasp the basics of repentance and forgiveness. Of course we still stumble, but as Peter teaches, there should be evidence of Jesus's influence on us through godly characteristics, evident in increasing measure. God longs to see us gallop through the surf of his grace, but to do that we need him to transform our minds.

Become Like Children

In "Jack and the Beanstalk," Jack is a boy. He sees the world through the eyes of a child. Jesus speaks of this childlike faith in Matthew 18:1-4:

> At that time the disciples came to Jesus and asked, "Who is the greatest in the kingdom of heaven?"
>
> Then he called a little child over to sit among the disciples, and said, "I assure you that if you don't turn your lives around and become like this little child, you will definitely not enter the kingdom of heaven. Those who humble themselves like this little child will be the greatest in the kingdom of heaven."

Become like children. This is key, and because it's key, the world has twisted the concept by idolizing children and vilifying the process of growing up. Children aren't the answer to the world's troubles, as some would have us believe. Why do we fall for that anyway?

I was a child once. I didn't have the answers. We all grew up surrounded by children, and many were barely capable of making it through recess without an altercation, never mind engineering world peace. Children certainly have the capacity for innocence, kindness, and selflessness, but they must be guided and nurtured since they also have the capacity for greed, meanness, and great folly. All of us began life as children, and it didn't take long for us to find the wide road to sinful choices. Why imagine a fresh crop will be any different?

One phrase from the Bible that contributes to this false notion that children contain the answers for society is from Isaiah 11:6:

> The wolf will live with the lamb,
> and the leopard will lie down with the young goat;
> the calf and the young lion will feed together,
> and a little child will lead them.

People repeat the last seven words out of context, as if to say that the wisest, purest leadership comes from children. Everyone oohs and nods as if it's the deepest wisdom of our world. That's not, however, what the passage teaches.

Isaiah 11 describes a day when the peace of Christ will rule. On that day, the peace will be so pervasive that a little child will be able to lead around a wolf and lion without fear of harm. It's not the leadership of the child that brings about peace but the righteousness of Christ. We spout nonsense about looking to the children for guidance or letting the church revolve around the children as if that will produce some great effect for the kingdom of God.

It's important to factor in the needs of children when making ministry decisions, but if my children had led our household, we'd have eaten nothing but goldfish crackers and spent our days playing Mario Kart. Revolving around childish Christians results in widespread spiritual immaturity and churches with ministries that look as though they're chasing soap bubbles in a meadow, not moving forward for God. This isn't to say that kingdom work is always linear or has an easily discernible pattern, but it should result in growth over time, not endless repetitions without signs of change.

Childlike or Childish

I've heard pastors preach the truth that Jesus, in Matthew 18, is exhorting us to be childlike, not childish. That's true. We don't grasp that concept, though, because unfortunately, while examples of childish behavior abound, we've relatively few examples of mature adults who have persevered with a childlike faith.

God has graciously allowed me to know saints like this. Through the years, older believers who exemplified maturity marked by childlike faith have guided and mentored me. I appreciate it now, but they exasperated me as an immature believer.

While others in the church had ready advice or knew a book I should read or plan I should follow, mature saints with childlike faith frequently had no clue what I should do about my latest dilemma. This was infuriating. They asked more questions than they answered and were prone to long pauses, as if listening to someone else while we chatted. Conversations with them looked more like this one I recall when I, as a college student, enjoyed an afternoon with Mr. B.

We sat together on a Sunday as his wife cleared the dinner dishes. He scanned the paper as I described my latest problem and the ensuing angst. After laying things out for him, I waited for wisdom. He looked at me, flashed a grin, and said, "Well, won't it be exciting for us to see what God's going to do with that one?"

"No," I answered. "Nothing about this feels exciting. Isn't there a Bible passage I should read or a prayer I should pray?"

He scowled, glancing up from the paper. "Have you stopped reading your Bible every day? Neglected prayer? Fallen into sin?"

"Of course not," I assured him. "I spend time with God, and I'm not sinning any more than usual."

Then he relaxed and leaned his head back. "Oh, well then, there's your answer. Maybe God thinks it's time for you to have an adventure. Pay attention and we'll see what we will see."

This type of maddening chat was typical of him, like having tea with the evangelical version of Willy Wonka. If I complained, Mrs. B. would chuckle and say, "He respects what God is doing in your life enough to stay out of the way when God's at work."

On those Sundays, Mr. B., who loved God's Word, didn't initiate Bible studies but he did initiate conversations about the importance of Sunday naps and not taking one's self too seriously. He didn't suggest evangelistic outings but instead encouraged me to learn the names of backyard birds. Once, after meeting my newest young man, Mr. B. suggested that, whereas he was clearly a nice fellow and quite serious about the Lord and life, I might want to reconsider my options. "You pray well together, but I don't think he's someone you're going to *play* well with for a lifetime."

"What does that even mean?" I asked.

"He's a bit of a stiff, dear," Mrs. B. said. "He's very fond of the sound of his own voice." (My husband, not the young man in question, will always be grateful for that particular conversation, as am I.)

Those Sunday chats imparted to me a sense of peace when trouble comes, the idea that God is at work in trials, a lasting notion that God has a plan for every tribulation, and a powerful understanding that God enjoys a spirit of joy and rest. Mr. B. never approached my problems with the message that I must have done something wrong to merit them or that I must follow a specific prescription to remedy them. His attitude was always that trouble is to be expected and is, in fact, an opportunity to watch God at work.

That's childlike faith, and I'll tell you what, it's contagious! The older Mr. B. grew, the lighter his step and the quicker his smile even though he saw plenty of life's troubles. I always had a sense that, somehow, he was in on God's secrets.

Friendship with God

Psalm 25:14 says, "The secret of the LORD is for those who fear Him, / And He will make them know His covenant" (NASB). The ESV translation says, "The friendship of the LORD is for those who fear him, and he makes known to them his covenant." The psalmist hints at an intimacy with God reserved for those who revere him. This is what I saw in Mr. B., and it made me hunger to experience it myself. That hunger did more to keep me from sin than all the stern warnings and programs offered by younger church leaders. Their attitudes made me nervous and fearful. Mr. B.'s settled me, secured me in Christ, and gave me courage.

My older friend was an obedient follower of Jesus. He studied God's Word, prayed, worshiped, fellowshipped regularly with believers, and served God in many ways. He grew up in Christ, and as he did, his sense of adventure, wonder, and complete trust in Christ grew as well. He exemplified childlike faith housed within an ordered, obedient life.

My friend Diane also matured in the Lord but retained her childlike faith. She was different from other believers at our conservative church. Diane was loud—really loud. She loved to host parties and had energy all the time. Being with Diane was like rolling with a pack of puppies. She had Christian friends, but she didn't hang with them as much as she hung with her karate friends and with struggling teens. God had sent her specifically to them so she could tell them about Jesus and demonstrate his love.

Diane was special to my daughter because when I mentioned that six-year-old Hannah was having panic attacks, Diane whisked her off to a karate class. It was a class for children, but Diane attended with Hannah and made her feel welcome, confident, and safe. While others suggested therapy or discipline, Diane, with her childlike perspective, helped Hannah find an out-of-the-box solution that worked for my active girl.

Other believers sometimes looked askance at Diane. She was rarely serious unless she was listening to a teen describe heartbreak or mastering a karate move. She laughed all the time and was forever on the go, saying yes to every crazy adventure that came her way. She loved God's Word, but she was no theologian. And did I mention she was loud?

Trusting God's Design

When Hannah was still six, we attended our first karate performance in a school gymnasium. She was quiet, nervous, and reserved. I hesitated to let her sit across the room with her friends, but she insisted. I was high up in the bleachers when the lights dimmed, and I saw Hannah panic at the dark. Her anxiety worsened when her friends abandoned her to sit in another section. I wondered how I would get to her, but then, above the music and applause, I heard Diane's loud "Woohoo!" as her son performed. Hannah heard it, too.

As if it were a game of Marco Polo, Hannah followed Diane's voice through the dark until she made it up onto her lap. She remained there for the rest of the performance. In that moment, I appreciated the way God had designed Diane. She always trusted God's idea of her, and that's what made her special. She was that voice in the darkness for many, right up until the day she died, too young, of cancer. Even through cancer, she trusted Jesus the way a child trusts her father as they drive through a dark tunnel. She spread the gospel of Jesus with every breath until she arrived in Glory.

It's challenging to cling to our childlike faith because it often leads us to color outside the lines of standard culture, even standard church culture. It doesn't lead us to sin or to extrabiblical teaching, but it does give us eyes to see ministries, needs, or approaches that others have never considered. This can be unsettling. Diane's outgoing nature wore me out and sometimes made me nervous, but I respected her confidence in Christ's love for her and her complete abandon to the work of building the kingdom of God. I adjusted to the discomfort and was better for it, but others tried endlessly to rein her in or calm her down to a muted version of God's design for her.

Craving Solid Food

The writer of Hebrews chides immature believers that there is much more to the faith experience than they're currently enjoying but that they're clinging to their baby faith. (I can almost hear the biblical writer shout, "You can't handle maturity!" That's my paraphrase. Here's the actual passage.)

> We have a lot to say about this topic, and it's difficult to explain, because you have been lazy and you haven't been listening. Although you should have been teachers by now, you need someone to teach you an introduction to the basics about God's message. You have come to the place where you

> need milk instead of solid food. Everyone who lives on milk is not used to the word of righteousness, because they are babies. But solid food is for the mature, whose senses are trained by practice to distinguish between good and evil. (Hebrews 5:11-14)

Breast milk or formula is perfect for infants, but if a growing adult tries to subsist on it, she lacks strength and mental clarity needed to meet the challenge of daily life. In other words, she's too weak for the adventure. This is where many of us find ourselves, but there is a remedy. We should consistently encourage one another to grow up.

Problem or Adventure?

In the fairy tale, Jack likely goes to bed with his mother's disappointment ringing in his ears. How could he believe the beans held any magic? She was all grown up. She knew what was what. Jack sleeps, but while he sleeps, life emerges from the beans.

Jack awakens to a beanstalk. He has no idea where it leads. He's never climbed a tall vine before. Jack's mother must see the stalk, too, but she doesn't climb. More likely she sees the vine as a problem; a giant weed in her yard leading to the clouds could only mean trouble as far as she could see. Jack sees an invitation to adventure.

Jack makes the climb. Despite his hunger, their famine, and his mother's scolding, Jack retains a childlike sense of curiosity and hope. Jack certainly matures as he climbs and grows up as he faces the giant, but his faith swells with him. Jack's mother's faith remains as dry as their cow's udder. Jack's faith bursts forth with life.

The New Testament writers call to us from higher up on the vine that is life in Jesus Christ. They beckon us, saying, *Good, you've found the vine! Don't remain at the spot where you encountered it! Come with us. Follow Jesus ever higher. Don't be afraid. Climb. We'll help you find the next handhold and the next.*

To place our faith in Jesus Christ, to embrace obedience to his Word, to trust him alone in a world full of lies, to renounce cynicism and self-protection in favor of hope and confidence in Christ: this is what it is like to become like children. To bury the beans in the soil of our lives and sleep, knowing God is at work in our souls, to wake and climb the living vine that emerges in order to topple giants: this is what it's like to have childlike faith in a world under the influence of dark forces. To trade in our cows that produce no milk for dried beans that contain life: this is the courage of children listening to their trustworthy Father and reaping the benefits of his care.

This childlike faith produces mature believers so grown up in Christ that they're capable of nurturing others. They're also capable of hearing how the world cries out for beans. It doesn't sound like what you'd think, but that's a conversation for the next chapter.

Small Steps Toward Slaying Giants

1. List behaviors and attitudes considered childish and list those considered childlike. Are there believers in your life who are examples of people growing up in Jesus while retaining a childlike faith? Ask one out for coffee. Get to know him or her and see what habits this person has that you can adopt.
2. Read Matthew 18:1-4. We call children *dependents* because they're completely dependent on their parents. Consider this as you read John 5:19-24 and 15:1-17. What does dependence on Jesus look like, and what is the result?
3. Look again at the list of giants you listed in chapter 1. Are any of those giants a result of childish behavior on your part? Are any a result of rejecting your own design? How could growing up in Jesus and embracing his design of you affect your perspective on those giants?
4. Read 1 Samuel 17. How did David's perspective on Goliath reveal maturity of faith greater than that of warriors who were older than David? How did David approach the battle in a way that showed he respected the way God had designed him?

One Stone for Your Sling: Jack was nothing without the vine.

8

How the World Cries Out for Beans

When disasters strike, rescuers rely on their ears to find people beneath the rubble. Recovery workers stop frequently so they can listen for the faintest cries. It's frustrating, labor-intensive, and tedious, but the people under the collapse are worth every effort. Rescuers fear abandoning people trapped just feet from salvation because no one heard them call out.

We live in disastrous times. The work of extricating people from the rubble of their lives is frustrating, labor-intensive, and tedious. Still, it's our calling to hear the cries of those longing to be located and rescued. One barrier to doing this is that not everyone calls out in a language we can understand. Not everyone says "Help me" as clearly as that.

Having had lupus, I know a single disease can manifest multiple ways. It requires a skilled physician to recognize when different symptoms are not many problems but evidence of a single problem. Without this wisdom, doctors might attempt to treat individual symptoms and worsen the health of the patient rather than cure him or her. Discerning the many ways our world manifests its soul-hunger is even more important.

To some, it appears humanity has multiple problems. Those lacking a biblical worldview attack each concern as if it stems from a varied source when truthfully there is often one culprit to blame. That culprit is our separation from God and our need to be reconciled through Jesus. Relying on the wrong course of treatment serves only to make matters worse and may delay the cure until hope is nearly lost.

Soul-Hunger Is Real

This isn't to say the straight-line cure to every problem is Jesus. Even after we enter into a relationship with Jesus we experience troubles, wrestle with sin, and suffer the results of living in a fallen world. Still, if a soul never comes to terms with his or her need for Jesus, it's likely the hunger gnawing at the person's soul will never quiet. Satisfying it will become a driver for behavior, choices, and mind-sets that contribute to an entire matrix of life worked out on a faulty grid. Soul-hunger is real. We can quell it temporarily with things that aren't healthy spiritual food, but we'll suffer from this counterfeit intake.

We're created beings. Behind our design is a brilliant engineer, artist, craftsman, and loving Father, all rolled up into one supreme being. He reveals the secrets of his design in his Word, the Bible. Through his Word, we learn we've been hard-wired to worship, create, be in community, and desire love. He devised us to engage imagination, to enjoy work, to appreciate beauty, and to communicate. We're adventurous, curious, inventive, and complex. Fashioned in his image, we're endlessly fascinating.

When we twisted our design through sin and our rejection of God, we didn't negate what he wrote into our original programs. We set a divide between God and us, a divide that Jesus had to bridge. Still, even lost, we retain the artist's signature, his thumbprint, his unique mark. That deep, inner code beeps like a homing device. It reminds us of our purpose, emerging in our output whether we plan for it to or not.

Paul says in Romans 1:18-20:

> God's wrath is being revealed from heaven against all the ungodly behavior and the injustice of human beings who silence the truth with injustice. This is because what is known about God should be plain to them because God made it plain to them. Ever since the creation of the world, God's invisible qualities—God's eternal power and divine nature—have been clearly seen,

> because they are understood through the things God has made. So humans are without excuse.

God is just. He surrounded us with testimony about himself, not only in creation but also in ourselves, his created beings.

The Unknown God

When Hannah was little, she spent an afternoon angry with me. At one point, she dragged my guitar into the kitchen and asked if I'd like to hear her new song. She strummed a pretend chord and sang, "This song is for my mom who doesn't understand me. She won't understand this song either, but even if she did, she still wouldn't understand me." Clumsy, yes, but effective art. We express our heart-cries through songs, poems, and drawings. Working with abused and neglected children, I'm careful to examine their artwork or compositions for messages.

Paul recognized this in Acts 17:22-28 when he addressed the people of Athens:

> Paul stood up in the middle of the council on Mars Hill and said, "People of Athens, I see that you are very religious in every way. As I was walking through town and carefully observing your objects of worship, I even found an altar with this inscription: 'To an unknown God.' What you worship as unknown, I now proclaim to you. God, who made the world and everything it is, is Lord of heaven and earth. He doesn't live in temples made with human hands. Nor is God served by human hands, as though he needed something, since he is the one who gives life, breath, and everything else. From one person God created every human nation to live on the whole earth, having determined their appointed times and the boundaries of their lands. God made the nations so they would seek him, perhaps even reach out to him and find him. In fact, God isn't far away from any of us. In God we live, move, and exist. As some of your own poets said, 'We are his offspring.'"

The apostle knew that something within humanity cries out for God, even a fallen culture that has rejected him. He knew to look to their art and their idols for signs of it. We're wise to do likewise. We can deny God. We can reject him outright. We can try to smother our need for him, outlaw him, ridicule him, banish him from our public forums, and run from him every day of our lives, but we can't escape our own design.

A Homing Device

In *Star Trek: The Next Generation*, Data is a remarkably human android. In Season 4, Episode 3, titled "Brothers," Data inexplicably hijacks the Starship *Enterprise* and returns to visit his creator, Dr. Noonien Soong. The doctor, facing his own death, had activated the homing device he'd placed in Data at his inception. Dr. Soong has a gift for Data, but unfortunately, Data's evil brother, Lore, also heeds the summons of the device implanted in his original code. Lore has nefarious plans for Dr. Soong's gift.

With this story line, the show's creator, Gene Roddenberry, and writer of this episode, Rick Berman, suggest an assumption that any creator with a relationship to his creation, even one that turned on him, would instill in that creation some mechanism by which the creator could call out and draw him or her back home.

God knew our sin would create a spiritual amnesia, a forgetting of who we are. He tagged our souls with his image so we would have inner flashes of remembrance that we were meant for more. We express these flashes, these hunger pangs of our souls through art, sending them up like flares.

Too often, Christians observe the world through a lens of judgment. There's a time and a place for discernment, especially when determining in which of the world's activities we might engage. But as Paul demonstrated in Athens, that's not the only biblical lens at our disposal. Paul didn't whip through downtown Athens destroying idols, even though he certainly understood the sinfulness of idols. Instead, he acknowledged the one dedicated to the unknown god as evidence the Grecians knew they were missing an important deity.

Meant for More

What happens when we survey our culture, art, pastimes, and fascinations with a view to learning what they say about the longing of human hearts?

What if, like Paul, we appropriate this information as an intersection at which we can meet our unsaved neighbors? What if we use these touch points to begin transformative conversations? What does humanity's output say about our soul-hunger? In other words, how does the world betray its own longing for beans?

Soul-hunger is visible in the stories we tell and the characters we create, especially the ones we repeat across generations and sometimes across cultures. Take giants, for example. We love to populate our stories with giants. Giants who terrorize and require defeating. Giants whom we tame. Giants aiming to subjugate us but whom we finally vanquish. We tolerate only gentle giants who bear a similarity to humans.

Humanity is hungry to overcome. Our treatment of the giants in our stories demonstrates this hunger. We recognize we're small but also that we have the capacity to be conquerors even when plagued by giants. God's heart for us is also that we become conquerors of giants, but he insists on being a factor in the equation. Romans 8:37-39 say: "But in all these things we win a sweeping victory through the one who loved us. I'm convinced that nothing can separate us from God's love in Christ Jesus our Lord: not death or life, not angels or rulers, not present things or future things, not powers or height or depth, or any other thing that is created."

From fairy tales to feature films, we also create commoners who learn they come from royalty. We hunger to know that we possess noble blood and inherit a regal lineage. Something within us points to this, cries out for this to be true. Even the real-life stories we gravitate to, such as Princess Diana's rise from nanny to princess, betray an inner whisper that we have the ability to lead the kingdom from which we've been separated. This couldn't be truer. In Christ, we learn we were predestined for adoption (Ephesians 1:5) by the king of all creation. We are destined to lead. We are children of a benevolent monarch.

Slavic children's tales flip this concept on its head while still illustrating a biblical truth. In these stories, the peasants star and teach peasant children they are the ones who are rich and wise, whereas those with power and gold are actually lacking. Something in us knows that what the world values is not of true worth and that the last will one day be first. African storytelling also features wise characters (one of whom often takes the form of a spider) to play out the theme of the small overcoming the powerful. Asian tales often reflect a value on an individual sacrificing himself or herself for the sake of all others. Hearts worldwide cry out for God.

The yearning that we were meant for more emerges in comic books, movies, and TV series featuring humans discovering hidden potential, such as superheroes. We hunger to believe we can be greater than we currently appear. This emerges not only in fiction but also in our fascination with the Olympics, professional sports, and record-setting. Scripture says we are capable in Christ. Nothing is impossible through him, and we cry out for this through our art.

Unleashing Our Potential

Pair this desire for superpowers with the profusion of stories about the supernatural and we see some of our cries aren't even subtle. We construct stories populated with otherworldly beings, dripping fascination with a parallel spiritual world. Our enchantment with vampires, angels, immortality, and time travel reveals that God placed eternity on our hearts (Ecclesiastes 3:11). We sense the presence of a spiritual realm even while rejecting a biblical understanding of it.

And what of our understanding that we need transformation? How does that emerge? Some networks devote their entire programming to individual, home, and business makeovers. The wide audience for these shows demonstrates that we know something is wrong with us. We understand our lives need an overhaul. Longing for transformation, we focus on the flesh instead of the spirit, attempting to accomplish the work ourselves rather than submit to Christ.

Then there's romance. We weave romance into every story, even seeking romantic angles to our news reports. God planted within us a love for romance that reflects his, as evidenced by his enchanting and extravagant creation. The moon, waterfalls, and roses were his idea. Our love of romance is his image within us, but again, we're aiming it in the wrong direction.

Explore the Mystery

Our desire for romance goes beyond finding a spouse. We also seek the romance of great quests. We embed adventures across genres and pursue them in real life through travel shows. Saint Augustine of Hippo said, "To fall in love with God is the greatest romance; to seek Him the greatest adventure; to find Him, the greatest human achievement."[1] God calls us to engage in the romance of his creation and to experience the adventure of a life in relationship with him. He tells us in 1 Corinthians 2:9-10: "This is precisely what is written: 'God has prepared things for those who love him that no eye has seen, or ear has heard, or that haven't crossed the mind of any human being.' God has revealed these things to us through the Spirit. The Spirit searches everything, including the depths of God." What an incredibly romantic, adventurous notion it is to search even the depths of God. He intends us to live this adventure, and something inside us knows this.

Our passion for mysteries, puzzles, problem-solving video games, and quest story lines all speak to our hidden desire to unravel the mysteries of God. We assemble assortments of characters who team together for these adventure quests, revealing our need for community. God hard-wired this need into our personalities to draw us to him and to his church.

Even less subtle, our obsession with food as evidenced by the proliferation of food shows—even entire food networks—screams of a hunger we sense that won't be quiet no matter what we consume! Jesus answers our hungry hearts with himself in John 6:35: "I am the bread of life. Whoever comes to me will never grow hungry, and whoever believes in me will never be thirsty." We won't satisfy this gnawing need apart from him.

The Star Wars franchise has enjoyed decades of popularity because it voices our hunger by expressing most of these elements in one story line:

adventure, romance, hidden royalty, heroics, immortality, the existence of a parallel world, and the team quest. Fairy tales endure from generation to generation because they give voice to all these hungers. From Shakespeare to Sorkin, writers exist who can hear our cries from beneath the rubble of a fallen world. While they translate those cries into stories and works of art, they don't always know the food that will satisfy and save, that is, Jesus Christ, the bread of life.

Christians know what the world cries out to receive. God calls us to hear them cry and to create responses they can hear in return. To be effective and fruitful in this, we must bury the beans and cling to the vine.

Small Steps Toward Slaying Giants

1. Some may be too tenderhearted to engage in a close examination of their culture. Believers who are new to the faith or easily susceptible to the temptation of culture may be wise to skip step 3. Mature believers gifted with wisdom, discernment, evangelism, and mercy, however, can benefit the faith community much as the men of Issachar served the nation of Israel: "Of Issachar, men who had understanding of the times, to know what Israel ought to do, 200 chiefs, and all their kinsmen under their command" (1 Chronicles 12:32 ESV). If you're tenderhearted, examine the fairy tales and children's stories that appeal to each generation to learn what themes echo through time.
2. All of us can pray that God raises workers for the harvest—workers who are willing to hear the cries of the unsaved and able to design responses to what they hear. More and more, this calls for creativity. Can you commit to praying regularly for writers, composers, filmmakers, choreographers, or playwrights who seek to communicate Christ to the unsaved? Reach out and ask how you can join their prayer teams.
3. Think about the people to whom God has called you. List what you know about what entertainment they consume. You don't need to watch or listen to these things yourself to know their themes. (In fact, sometimes that would be a mistake.) Check Internet sites that summarize books, movies, TV shows, and lyrics. Or ask them to describe their entertainments and what they find appealing. Pray for openness to their hearts and for eyes to see the themes of their soul-hunger. Pray for a deeper understanding of their needs. Outreach isn't a one-size-fits-all endeavor. While everyone seeking to minister should know Scripture, pray, obey Christ, and yield to his Spirit, the actual work translates differently. A ministry to children in the suburbs of Kansas may look radically different from a ministry to bikers in San Francisco. Think about one aspect of modern culture you enjoy—a popular song,

sports team, play, graphic novel, or movie. What does this interest reveal about the cry of your heart? How does God answer that cry for you? Could this be a connecting point for you with others who share this interest but who don't know Jesus?

One Stone for Your Sling: We can deny God. We can reject him outright. We can try to smother our need for him, outlaw him, ridicule him, banish him from our public forums, and run from him every day of our lives, but we can't escape our own design.

PART 3

Clinging to the Vine

You must be doers of the word and not only hearers who mislead themselves.

James 1:22

In Part 3, each quality receives its own six-day ministudy with both information and inspiration. **Day 1** provides information, Scripture references, and both biblical and historical role models of that quality. **Days 2–5** offer inspirational essays on an aspect of living these qualities. **Day 6** encourages a day of reflection and suggests activities for fostering this quality individually and in community. To allow a day to rest from all your labors, there's no Day 7. No one masters these qualities in one week, but these chapters provide a launch pad for growth.

9

FAITH BURIES THE BEANS

Faith

Day One

Are you ready to bury the beans?

It takes faith to believe a dried-up bean contains life, which is why Peter makes sense when he tells us the process of being effective and fruitful in our knowledge of Christ begins with faith.

If I hand you a sack of beans and tell you it contains enough protein to feed your family but you must bury them in the ground and wait, you need faith to follow through, especially if you've never seen food grow. In the same way, millions of people know the story of Jesus and his sacrifice for them, but unless the gospel "seed" takes root in their hearts through faith, it's like a sack of dry beans left unused on a pantry shelf (Matthew 13:1-23).

Pursuing a black belt in karate after forty years of sedentary living required a leap of faith. To onlookers it was a fool's endeavor, and even to me it appeared impossible. Two things ignited my faith. The first was that God had clearly orchestrated the situation. I was leading a Bible study for black-belt women. We met after their karate class. Even if it took the rest of my life to earn a belt, God had called me to try.

The second thing was that the instructors and advanced students assured me what I was attempting was possible. Whenever I complained I'd never reach black belt, every person countered, "You will attain it if you persevere." Their faith—in the process, in perseverance, and in God's ability to keep me going—encouraged me to press on, so at forty-four I earned the rank of first-degree black belt. It began with faith, but I couldn't just believe from the chairs at the side of the room. For all the ladies' encouragement, I had to put faith into action by suiting up and joining them on the mats.

Rooted in Faith

Faith is essential, so it merits a thorough exploration. God sows the word widely throughout Scripture. So much so, we skim over it as if it's a spiritual punctuation mark our minds barely register. *Faith* is the kind of word we assume we understand until we read a verse like Matthew 17:20, where Jesus said, "I assure you that if you have faith the size of a mustard seed, you could say to this mountain, 'Go from here to there,' and it will go. There will be nothing that you can't do."

After we read that, we think, okay, maybe I don't understand faith. Because I'm not moving mountains, slaying giants, or even motivating myself to ask my new neighbors in for coffee. This is the moment when, if you're like me, you hope the secret to understanding faith lies in knowing the Greek.

The Greek word Peter uses is *pistis,* meaning conviction of truth in anything, belief. According to James Strong, it derives from the root word *peitho,* meaning persuade, to be persuaded, to trust, have confidence, be confident.[1]

As I write this, the chorus of the hymn, "I Know Whom I Have Believed," rings in my ears: "I know whom I have believed, and am persuaded that He is able, to keep that which I've committed unto Him against that day."[2]

I recall singing that hymn with conviction as a child. Whenever our congregation belted it out, we left church fortified. Any doubts that had attached to our souls during the week, like burrs from a nature hike, fell away, and with each chorus we grew more confident.

Confident in Jesus

Faith is belief. Trust. Confidence. Full persuasion that a thing is true. Faith in Jesus Christ is belief, trust, confidence, full persuasion in the person and work of Jesus. Every believer must start with faith. The writer of Hebrews declares this: "Without faith it is impossible to please him, for whoever would draw near to God must believe that he exists and that he rewards those who seek him" (Hebrews 11:6 ESV).

This passage stimulates my desire for faith because I want to please God. It also clarifies why the enemy expends much energy attacking these two areas of faith. Satan's tempting us either to doubt God exists or, if that doesn't work, to doubt God's goodness in order to drain our faith reserves.

Faith Interrupted

When my kids were young, Zack took swim lessons at the YMCA. Hannah watched him for two years and was eager to be old enough for her own class. When the day arrived, however, she balked poolside. Suddenly she was a puddle of tears at the thought of entering the water. My son's impish expression gave me the clue about what to ask: "Did Zack say anything about swimming?"

My four-year-old nodded. "He told me watch out for the big drain at the bottom because sometimes they pull the plug and little kids get sucked right down. No one can ever find them."

Fortunately, Hannah was able to draw on her faith in me and her faith in what she'd witnessed for two years to overcome the seed of doubt her devious brother had planted. She became a happy swimmer. But this scenario plays out in our Christian lives all the time.

For example, we pray and nothing happens. We pray again, to no avail. People in our lives (or voices appearing as thoughts) offer this unanswered prayer as evidence that there is no God or that he's a God who doesn't care what happens in our little lives. This attack is a direct shot at faith, an attempt to cripple us on a foundational level. The battle against faith is fierce, which is why we need to continue always to grow, to have faith in "increasing measure" (2 Peter 1:8 ESV).

Peter wrote his letter to believers, people who had begun the journey with God in faith. As you'll recall, he opened with this greeting: "Simeon Peter, a servant and apostle of Jesus Christ, to those who have obtained a faith of equal standing with ours by the righteousness of our God and Savior Jesus Christ" (2 Peter 1:1 ESV). Other translations use the word *received* rather than *obtained*, which is closest to the Greek word *lagchano*, which means "to receive by divine allotment."[3] Faith starts with God and is a gift from God. It's the spark that lights our way to the truth of Jesus when we're still standing in the darkness of sin. Faith is the platform, the launch pad, our sure footing for progressing forward into these other characteristics, which will ensure we're effective and fruitful in our knowledge of Jesus Christ.

Steps to Action

I'm not a pastor or a Bible expert. I write these chapters from the perspective of a well-studied layperson. I also write from the perspective of a woman who's spent more than fifty years reading and studying God's Word, living it in the trenches, and walking with Jesus.

When I sense the prompting of the Lord to grow in a certain area or to overcome a character weakness, I approach the challenge by taking the following steps.

1. Study what Scripture has to say about the subject.
2. Pray about those Scriptures and request God's power over that area of my life. John 5:19 quotes Jesus saying, "I assure you that the Son can't do anything by himself except what he sees the Father doing. Whatever the Father does, the Son does likewise." Then Jesus tells us in John 15:5 that we can't do anything without him: "If you remain in me and I in you, then you will produce much fruit. Without me, you can't do anything."
3. Write or memorize key verses to fortify my efforts to change.

4. Seek role models who exemplify the change I need. I usually find biblical role models, historical ones, and at least one contemporary.
5. Trust God to work and to lead me into the growth he desires. Pay attention to the life lessons or training he provides when he's inspiring the growth. In other words, I keep my eyes open.
6. Invite other Christians to hold me accountable, pray for me, and encourage me as I pursue maturity in that area.

One cautionary reminder: none of this effort is about earning salvation. Salvation is by faith alone that no one can boast (Ephesians 2:8-9). Nor is it about earning an easy life or a favorable answer to every prayer. Godly men and women, loved by God and mature in the faith, face suffering, distress, persecution, and pain every day.

Mark 10:29-30 has this promise and warning for people of faith: "Jesus said, 'Truly, I say to you, there is no one who has left house or brothers or sisters or mother or father or children or lands, for my sake and for the gospel, who will not receive a hundredfold now in this time, houses and brothers and sisters and mothers and children and lands, with persecutions, and in the age to come eternal life'" (ESV).

The blessing we receive for following Jesus comes also with persecutions, which, if we have faith to accept them, can also be a blessing. No matter how full of faith we are, trouble will still come to those who love Jesus.

Through Jesus, we've received salvation and full daughter- and son-ship in the family of God. We're loved, accepted, and secure even when we fail. Growing in the qualities Peter describes is about moving toward greater effectiveness and fruitfulness for Jesus Christ and for furthering his kingdom.

Know the Goal

Knowing the goal can help us set realistic expectations that prevent discouragement. Spiritual growth is often more of a spiral motion than a straightforward line. All growth has seasons, and one of those seasons is dormancy, when it appears to onlookers as if nothing is occurring. This is why we need to restrain ourselves from judging others (Romans 14:4) and even from judging ourselves (1 Corinthians 4:3); we need simply apply ourselves to following Jesus, to studying and obeying his word, and to prayer. If we keep our focus on Christ and find our motivation in what God's Word promises, it will prevent us from abandoning our efforts when opposition arises or hardships come.

Rather than the "boring bean" it appears to be, faith as described in God's Word is ripe with life and possibility for change.

Word Study Exercise

Find the following Gospel passages and consider what they say about faith:

Faith can be small: Matthew 6:30, Matthew 8:23-27
Faith can be great: Matthew 8:5-13, Matthew 15:21-28
Faith can be absent: Matthew 17:14-21, Mark 4:35-41
Faith is made visible through action: Matthew 9:2, Luke 7:36-50
Faith is active in healing: Matthew 9:1-8, Matthew 9:18-26, Matthew 9:27-31, Mark 10:46-52
Faith can be impeded by doubt: Matthew 14:22-33, Matthew 21:18-22
Faith can fail: Luke 22:31-34
Small faith is all that is needed to do great things: Matthew 17:20
Faith can grow: Luke 17:5-6

What do these passages tell you or remind you about faith?

With whom do you most identify in the stories?

(If you identify with the unbelieving crowd in the passages, this may be the moment God is calling you to cross over into faith in Jesus Christ. If you're studying with a group, ask one of the believers to pray with you as you accept Jesus's sacrifice for your sins. If you're reading on your own, simply pray to Jesus that you realize you're a sinner and you believe he died to pay for your sins. Ask him to lead you into his salvation and to direct you to people who can guide you.)

The sense I get from those passages is that faith can shrink or expand. While faith comes from God, once we believe and are in relationship with Jesus, we play a pivotal role in the dynamics of our faith. Jesus repeatedly chides the disciples with the phrase, "O you of little faith." It's not the stern warning he uses with unbelievers in Matthew 17:17, referring to them as a "faithless and crooked generation," but it's a challenge that their faith could grow, their trust in Jesus could be greater because Jesus is worthy of all trust and every confidence.

The more we know him, the more we observe him at work, the greater confidence we should have that he is worthy of our faith. How has your faith grown through the years? What is the evidence of faith in your life? 

You'll find faith is one of Paul's favorite topics. He teaches that some are weak in faith and others are strong, but the apostle warns we aren't to judge one another over the expanse of our faith (Romans 14), especially because we can have all faith but if we don't have love, we are nothing (1 Cor. 13). Some have a special spiritual gift of faith, having been proportioned from God with a generous measure (Romans 12:3), but we all have some faith. We can encourage one another's faith (Romans 1:12), and our faith can increase (2 Corinthians 10:15).

Faith Is a Muscle

Taken as a whole, these passages describe faith that is like the sturdy heart muscle of our walk with Christ. We refer to some people as having "big hearts," meaning they're more loving or generous than others, but we understand everyone needs a beating heart in order to be alive. In the same way, even though some may have greater faith, we all need a "beating" faith in order to have a spiritual pulse. Just as exercise is recommended in any good cardiac regimen, so the exercise of our faith results in a healthier faith muscle.

Biblical Role Model Ministudy

It helps to know what faith looks like when it's dressed in flesh and blood, isn't it? For that, we need to see humans exhibiting faith. I take encouragement from the fact that the disciples began with "little" faith. Read Matthew 26:69-75, then Acts 4:1-22. What is the difference in Peter in these two stories? What factors made this difference?

Read Hebrews 11 and make a list of the men and women of faith listed there. Take special note of 11:32-40. What do these verses tell us about faith as a protection from trial and suffering?

Now choose one or two of the people mentioned here and read their stories in the Old Testament. My favorites are Noah (Genesis 6–9; Hebrews 11:7; 1 Peter 3:20; 2 Peter 2:5), Abraham and Sarah (Genesis 12–25; Romans 4; Galatians 3:6-18; Hebrews 6:13-20), or Gideon (Judges 6–8).

As you read, ask questions. How did their faith manifest itself in their lives? How did they respond to God? To challenges? To opposition? To disappointments? To blessing? How am I like them? How am I different?

Heritage of Faith Walkers

List Christians whose faith you admire from history or from your own life. How does faith manifest itself in their lives? How do they respond to God, to challenges, to opposition, to disappointments, to blessings?

Can't think of any Christians from history known for their great faith? One you could research is George Mueller (1805–1898), Christian evangelist and director of the Ashley Down orphanage in Bristol, England. Mueller was known for his reliance on God through expectant prayer. Others include Amy Carmichael, Watchman Nee, Hudson Taylor, Jim Elliot, Elisabeth Elliot, and Rochunga Pudaite. Ask others from your faith community and start a list. Choose one who particularly inspires you and look at the faith practices he or she incorporated into daily life. Incorporate at least one of those into yours.

Whom do you know who exhibits great faith? What about his or her life testifies to that faith? Do you know his or her story? Plan to meet this person for coffee or a meal and ask about the history of his or her faith. What counsel does he or she have for others—for you in particular—to grow in faith?

Small Steps Toward Slaying Giants

1. Choose a passage from one of those you just studied to read every day this week. Try to memorize it, but also ask God to show you what this verse looks like applied in your life right now. Record his answer and then put it into practice.
2. What thoughts did this chapter spark about the dynamics of your faith? Consider drawing a simple timeline of your life by decades (or years if you're under thirty). At what points was your faith strong? Weak? What factors contributed to each? Where is your faith now? Where would you like it to be next year? What in the lives of the faith-filled people you studied contributed to their faith overcoming harsh circumstances? How can you incorporate that understanding in your life this week?

One Stone for Your Sling: Faith buries the beans.

Faith

Day Two

When the World Runs Out of Tears

A Declaration of Faith

The essays accompanying each characteristic will vary in style because each of us finds inspiration through various means. This first is a declaration of faith through a prayer of lament.

When the world runs out of tears because we can weep no more—
Because the body counts are becoming just more numbers—
Because those cut down are a different color, country, gender, politic, or faith—
Because one murder follows another and our hearts have no time to rehydrate—
When the world runs out of tears for the dead, Lord, you still know their names, the idea you had when you designed each one, their promise, and your potential within them.
You know where each one fell, and how, and by whose hand. They never really died alone or unwitnessed. The crimes against them, you record to be revealed on that day.
When the world runs out of tears, you still have compassion for the recent dead.

(based on Matthew 10:26-33; Genesis 4:10)

When justice is a punch line, a footnote in history, preserved for private viewing only in a museum of ancient history,
When justice is so rare it's reserved for those with the right skin,

heritage, geography, connections, and cash,
When the nations discard justice along the side of the narrow road and place their faith instead in mob rule, revenge, or power they're promised in the dark,
When parents tell their children justice is a fairy tale as they nurse them with bitter milk,
You will remain the only righteous judge, the eternal process, the one who holds justice in his hands. You will remember, better than we, every life that was stolen, every bone that was broken, every innocence penetrated, every womb violated, every tooth shattered, every blood splattered, every hope scattered.
There will be a great gettin' up morning when holy justice is the only item on the menu for the day, for you will see that that sun rises in its time.

(based on Genesis 9:5-6; 1 Corinthians 4:5; 2 Peter 3:10-13)

When we finally blind ourselves because we cannot, will not, dare not see another lifeless child, another kidnapped daughter, another young man shot through, another old man severed, another weeping mother, or another orphaned babe
Because our hearts are fragile
Because our minds rebel against the horror
Because we can find no answers within ourselves
Because our eyes are scabbed from scraping our hands across them in the agony of more front-page art,
When we're finally blind, you will still see. Nothing escapes your vision, your scope, the reach of your right arm.
There is no darkness so dense your eyes cannot penetrate. Your laser focus sees them scurry like cockroaches from the true Light. You know where they hide. There need be no other witness on that day of holy reckoning because you know where all the bodies lie and

by your power, they will rise to testify against those who stole their light, their blood, their lives. You are the eternal irrefutable Witness.

When our love runs cold and we no longer have the heart to connect with another human who may die and leave us bereft,
When we are calloused and hardened from too many coffins,
When our arms no longer reach out to strangers, weakened by loss, by fear, by the weight of our cynicism,
When our minds, numbed by mass graves and headline tallies, lock up as if that were some protection from the pain,
When we are at risk of losing our own souls,
You will be our source, our wellspring, our ever-rich supply of Love Come Down, of Love Divine, of Love Excelling, of Love Never-Ending. You are love that lays down its life, love that lifts, amazes, runs like a river from soul to soul. You will be the love we need to survive a murderous age and not simply survive but to rise above and carry on
Despite the fallen in Kenya, the tortured in North Korea, the beaten in China, the exploited in Bangkok, the kidnapped in Nigeria, or the beheaded in Syria,
Despite the slaughtered, the aborted, the trafficked, the gunned-down, the poisoned, the missing, the murdered, the silenced, and the dead,
Despite every horror and agony that befalls us on our way home to you,
Your love will fill us. Your grace is sufficient. The dragon roars and snuffs out as many as he dares before your return, but he knows too well death won't win, murderers will be called to account, those who overcome will see your face and live forever.
And when we are prostrate before you,
kneeling bedside,
standing hands raised,
seeking your face,

we pray, O Lord, you will search our hearts and pluck from them the murderous seeds of anger against our brothers, seeds of unforgiveness, of selfishness, of greed, of quarreling, and of lust before our hearts, too, become hotbeds of murderous intentions that give rise to words that give thoughts to plans that give arms to action and we also fall prey to the homicidal spirit of this age.

Without you, we would be found with blood on our hands when you return as well.

But by your blood, we're washed clean, even if we barely remember what that looks like, surrounded by headlines that scream "Cain's ancestors rule, and Abel will never rise."

We know the truth. We wait to rise at your Word, O Lord, at your command. All who have fallen will rise on that day, at your say.

Only say the Word, and we shall be healed.

(based on 2 Thessalonians 1:5-10; James. 2:12-13;
2 Corinthians 12:9-10; Romans 8)

Small Steps Toward Slaying Giants

1. Shocking headlines can challenge or erode our faith. Some people choose to remain ignorant of world events. If we do that, how can we intercede? Others immerse themselves in the news, but this can lead to a skewed perspective, too. Write down one or two of the passages mentioned in the chapter to keep beside you when you watch the news. Read them often to remind yourself God remains in control.
2. Limit the amount of news you consume to what you can prayerfully handle. Try watching the news only with family or over coffee with friends. Or take notes in your prayer journal and schedule your news watching prior to your prayer time.

❧ ❧ ❧

One Stone for Your Sling: When the world runs out of tears, God still has compassion for the recent dead.

Faith

Day Three

The Trouble with an Invisible King

Following in Faith

You are sitting innocently (or perhaps not so innocently) in a worship service on the Thursday before Easter just minding God's business when the worship leader gives a simple instruction: "Take this time to examine your heart before the Lord in preparation for communion."

Nothing out of the ordinary. You've heard this instruction countless times through years. You don't anticipate any lightning bolts.

God surprises.

As you contemplate while simultaneously wondering how long your leader can tolerate silence, you hear a quiet voice within you ask, "Why do you demand from me another king?"

One simple question.

A question that brings your soul to its knees before God in that room, in that church basement that smells like a hundred years of coffee and modeling clay. A whisper from the Holy Spirit. He sees it. He's named it. He's brought it to your attention, the sin to which you cling.

The question is not out of context for the evening. Earlier the preacher instructed the gathered on the meaning of the Passover Seder. He walked you through the deliverance of Israel from Egypt all the way to the Promised Land. He touched on Israel's demand for a king (1 Samuel 8)—a king like ones all the other nations had. A king people could see.

With all the experience of God's provision and protection behind them, his kingship should have been enough. The Hebrew word for this, he explains, is *dayenu,* meaning "It would have been enough for us" or "It would have sufficed."[4] The Israelites should have been content with him as their king (*dayenu*). But no. They demanded a king everyone could see. God told Samuel to give them that for which they'd asked.

It's not always a good thing when God does that.

Short memories, you and the Israelites have. How quickly they forgot what happened in the wilderness when they whined and complained about subsisting on manna. They cried out for meat, and God sent them meat. He vowed they would eat meat until it came out their ears. He flooded them with quail and they ate, but it came with sickness, too, and death. The fallout of ingratitude.

Now you can see how you, too, have been demanding a king like everyone else.

For all your life, God has provided for your needs, but it comes like manna—just enough and just when you need it. You've been looking around at others. These others have storehouses of manna. They have bank accounts, stock portfolios, long-range financial plans, promised dividends, and IRAs. So, you've been thinking, why shouldn't you get some of that?

Yes, God has provided. (*Dayenu*)

Yes, God has always heard your prayers. (*Dayenu*)

Yes, you have food, shelter, clothing, and this should be enough. (*Dayenu*)

Still, you envy the deals others have brokered. You look at their visible kings and think, *I have got to get me one of those.*

In this silence, you realize how close you came to God's answering your request. You repent of that foolish prayer and thank him for giving you the opportunity to take it back before he gives you a king like everyone else.

The mercy of conviction.

Jesus is your king, and truly you desire no other. Jesus is your security, your money in the bank, your investment portfolio, your retirement plan, your hope chest, your inheritance. He is like no other.

You sympathize with Israel's envy of visible kings. It must have been hard to hear taunts from their enemies. *Show us your king! Bring him out! Where is your fierce leader? Oh, right, he's invisible, isn't he? No, no, that's soooo scary! We're terrified of your invisible king.*

And when you think of the taunts they would have received from the enemy, you recognized the voice of the evil one, the voice you've been hearing in your own thoughts, thoughts you then translated into ungrateful, demanding prayers.

You are undone before the Lord.

Thank God for mercy. Thank God for Jesus's death on the cross. Thank God for his resurrection. Thank God that he included you in his family through Jesus Christ, the only High King.

It will be hard, but you're no longer asking for a visible king, one like everyone else has. By the power of Jesus Christ, you will be content with manna, content with a king so real this world isn't ready to lay eyes on him. But one day, you and everyone else will see him.

No king but King Jesus. This is your Easter resurrection prayer.

Small Steps Toward Slaying Giants

1. Read Numbers 11, 1 Timothy 6:6-10, and Philippians 2:14-16. How seriously does God take complaining, grumbling, and ingratitude? How would content, uncomplaining, grateful people stand out in your community? What kind of impact would it make if the people in your church daily demonstrated contentment and uncomplaining gratitude? Why?
2. Can you relate to the Israelites? How hard is it to follow an invisible God? Money is a visible idol in our society, and it can be challenging to pursue God instead of financial success. What other idols are tempting to pursue? How can 1 Timothy 6:11-16 inspire you to carry on when it's hard?

One Stone for Your Sling: Jesus is your security, your money in the bank, your investment portfolio, your retirement plan, your hope chest, your inheritance. He is like no other.

Faith

Day Four

Worshiping in Reverse

Worshiping in Faith

On Sunday, one of our worship songs interfered with my worship.

It was unfamiliar. It sounded new—even to the musicians. They placed it right in the middle of the worship set, and I wondered why. It had lots of words and an awkward rhythm. Instead of focusing on God, I focused on the song choice. For several moments, I lost my worship flow.

Flash forward to the sermon. Our pastor preached on God's work in our lives through trial, then introduced a young mother of three who sported a bandana. This mom told her faith story. She testified about God's faithfulness to her family through her battle with stage 4, metastasized breast cancer. A powerful tale of God's provision and miraculous healing, her story mesmerized us.

As she concluded, she referenced a song, a family favorite, their theme song of faith through this trial. Of course, this was the unfamiliar song that had disrupted my worship earlier. As soon as I learned why we'd sung the song, I worshiped in reverse. The revelation was powerful and moving and drew me into the presence of God retroactively.

Strange, yes?

When I was meditating on what had happened, I latched onto a thought I couldn't shake. What if the first ten thousand years of our worship in eternity is simply the experience of us collectively worshiping retroactively?

Think about it. When we're there, all at once, we're going to see it—everything that came before, everything we didn't appreciate, or understand, or missed—through eyes that now see him face-to-face. Everything we've heard—every piece of Scripture, every sermon, hymn, praise song, testimony, word of exhortation, and every life event—will now click in a cosmic and collective *Aha* that will require a response.

We'll worship for his deliverance in our pasts, and it will likely extend for at least ten thousand years.

How could we not? All at once, we'll see the ways he protected us when we didn't even see the danger. We'll know every reason he denied certain prayers and all the answers to the ones we offered in faith. We'll hear his laughter, see his smile, know the light in which he cloaks himself, and we'll wrap ourselves in his great love, which we'll see was with us from before any of us saw light.

And we'll see ourselves in his light—how often we missed him, didn't recognize him, took him for granted, sold him out to others, ignored his grace. We'll see the moments that he sought us and bore with us when we blew him off. We'll understand, on the deepest level, his great patience, his heart, his persistence in pursuit, and his passion for our redemption.

What will stop us from falling on our knees, on our faces, for ten thousand years? We'll worship retroactively for his plan that preexisted our creation and endured into eternity.

Small Steps Toward Slaying Giants

1. Read Revelation 7:9-17 and 21:1-4, 22-27. Think of these scenes in light of 1 Corinthians 13:8-13. How can knowing this is our future inspire today's faith?
2. Can you think of a time when you thought one way about a situation until new information changed your perspective? What circumstances challenge you today? Ask God to help you see the circumstances from his perspective. Trust him for the day when you will worship in reverse.

❧ ❧ ❧

One Stone for Your Sling: What if the first ten thousand years of our worship in eternity is simply the experience of our collectively worshiping retroactively?

Faith

Day Five

Why Didn't We Believe More When It Mattered?

Acting in Faith

Tears streamed down the face of the woman coming toward me. "Lori, can you come help the man in my office?"

As we walked, she explained that he had lost the right to see his family and no one had given him a chance to address the things that caused the problem in the first place. He clearly needed help, but no one had offered it. It certainly sounded like a tragedy.

When we turned the corner to her office, I saw another woman nodding, patting the man's arm, and reaching for tissues. The man had his head down and his hand over his eyes. As we entered, he looked up, and our eyes met. When I spoke his name, his countenance changed immediately. "Oh, it's you," he said with a scowl.

"Yup, it's me," I replied. "Have you been telling these ladies no one gave you any chances to change? No one offered assistance? There was no way you could have seen this day coming? Is that what you've been saying?"

"Yeah," he replied, glancing at the women.

"Would you like me to tell them the number of times you were warned this day would come? The number of services, supports, and help you were offered but rejected? The number of people who reached out to you to convince you to take the warnings seriously before it was too late?"

"Hey! It's not my fault. Lots of people say things they don't mean and promise stuff that doesn't happen."

"Except this time, these people did mean what they said, their promises did come about, and you did choose to ignore all the warnings. Isn't that what's actually occurred?"

He nodded.

"Would you like help now?"

"What good would that do? It won't change anything."

"It would be a change for you. It would start you in the right direction for a healthier life."

"No, forget it. There's nothing wrong with me. It's you people." He walked out.

We all do this sometimes—ignore warnings. That's how we get caught on the beach in thunderstorms or in harmful relationships we could have avoided.

Sometimes, good people ignore warning signs because they're too terrible to believe. Women don't want to believe their husbands could be unfaithful. Parents don't want to know their children have developed addictions. Patients delay treatment hoping they're simply overly anxious about early symptoms. We dismiss rumors of war because the acts whispered in the wind are too dreadful to imagine.

I think about this when stories emerging from Syria flicker across my newsfeed. I don't click on them because they look like supermarket tabloids, too horrendous to be true. When the same stories appear in credible news sources, I cling to such modifiers as "some reports say" or "unverified sources," telling myself the truth will never be that bad, surely it won't.

Then I remember how I used to judge Westerners who lived through World War II. There were early reports out of Germany. Unverified sources told of persecutions, relocations, Jewish ghettos, and even the camps, but people couldn't accept that the reports were true. How could they be? The truth would never be that catastrophic. Right?

Except eventually, we learned the truth was worse.

We also tune out warning signs because we believe the lie that there's nothing we can do.

If we had the ear of a world power, we wouldn't feel as helpless, would we? We'd schedule regular conversations with this person. We'd advocate for action. We'd intercede for intervention. We'd petition for comfort and aid. We'd persist in making appeals until we saw results.

We do have the ear of a world power, the creator of the world power. We know those conversations by another term: prayer.

This is the age to believe what God says about prayer and about the spiritual battle raging around us. One day we'll stand with those who suffered, and they'll tell stories of miracles that occurred. God will connect the dots for us between those miracles and the prayers of others who didn't even know those who suffered.

On that day we'll cry out (until God banishes tears), Why didn't we pray more? Why didn't we believe the warning, the call to prayer? For the sake of our suffering brothers and sisters. For the sake of the threat marching toward our own door. For the sake of enemies who may have been converted before judgment day. Why didn't we believe more when it mattered?

In 2 Peter 3, Peter writes how the world scoffs at the warning that one day Jesus will return to judge us. They ignore every warning.

Peter tells us that God isn't slow to act. He's giving us a chance to bring as many aboard the ark of salvation as will come. Peter graciously instructs us how we are to live through these times, how we should hold on and not become unstable ourselves as the ship of this world lurches from side to side in the wake of the warnings God sends through his mercy.

Discover prayer, loved one. Pay attention to the times. Heed the warnings found in God's Word and intercede without ceasing for those who don't. Wage war on behalf of the suffering through constant prayer. Press into Jesus.

When we all gather before God at the end of the age, we'll want to know that we did all we could with the faith and gifts we were given. We'll want to know we believed and acted when it really mattered.

Small Steps Toward Slaying Giants

1. Read 2 Peter 3. What is God warning us will happen in the last days? Why is he slow to return? How does that demonstrate his love for humanity?
2. Read Ephesians 6:10-20. What does this passage teach about prayer? If you're not in the habit of a regular prayer time, schedule one each day this week. In what ways does your prayer life need to grow, deepen, expand, or mature?

❧ ❧ ❧

One Stone for Your Sling: This is the age to believe what God says about prayer and about the spiritual battle raging around us.

Faith

Day Six

Pray, Reflect, Process, Pray

Too many of us have adopted the culture of consumerism rather than the culture of discipleship. We come to books about our faith in a fashion that leads us to consume them rather than prayerfully and thoughtfully digest them. I've prayed better things for you, dear reader.

Growing up in Jesus is not a one-size-fits-all endeavor. We are climbing the true vine, and only he knows precisely where any one of us is in that process. Finding the next hold on the vine is not an exact science because it's about a relationship with Jesus, not a nine-step self-improvement program. Building character doesn't happen because we read we should do it. God builds character in us in many ways and through a variety of circumstances.

Here are my suggestions for today:

Ask God to direct you to activities that will give you faith in increasing measure. One way we bolster one another's faith is through testimonies or stories of God's intervention. Invite some friends for dinner and swap stories of times you've seen God at work.

Reflect on what you've read in his Word this week. Return to passages that spoke to where you are or inspired you to grow. Reread and reflect.

Everyone processes differently. Some do their best thinking while engaging in physical activity like running, washing the car, building a birdhouse, cleaning, or lifting weights. Others process through creative means such as journaling, painting, sculpting, writing, dancing, composing, or crafting. Still others process best by talking things through, either by chatting over coffee, spoken word poetry, monologue, or video. After you've reflected on your chosen Bible passage, engage in your preferred activity with the intent of processing what God has said to you through it about faith.

When you're done, ask God to continue the work of building your faith in increasing measure.

Now, lather, rinse, repeat. In other words, if this works for you, do it with other passages on faith or sections of the book that spoke to you.

10

Virtue from the Ground Up

Virtue

Day One

My friend lived in a pretty country home. She'd designed a lovely living room that was comfortable, inviting, and tastefully decorated. She'd chosen a delicate floral wallpaper that had held up nicely through the years. She enjoyed sitting in her favorite chair in that treasured room with a book and a cup of tea.

And then one day, she heard the crunching.

As she became aware of the sound, she wondered when it had started. When she told her husband, at first he thought she was crazy. It took weeks before he acknowledged that he, too, heard something. Was it crunching? Maybe it was a branch on the roof. Or the wind. It must be the pipes or heat coming up through the system. Before her husband heard it, she'd had her ears checked. Some people hear ringing; maybe she heard crunching.

She couldn't hear this noise in other parts of the house, only the living room. Initially it was faint and she didn't hear it all the time, but as the weeks passed, it became continuous and grew louder. The couple spent hours trying to locate the exact source, but they couldn't pin it down.

One night, she felt certain she'd go mad if she didn't identify what was crunching. She walked around the room, noting where it seemed loudest. At last she thought she'd located it just above the doorframe closest to her favorite chair. She dragged the step stool from the kitchen to the lovely living room and stood on the first step. Then, as she climbed higher, she reached above the doorframe and laid a hand on the wall to steady herself.

Except there was no wall.

Her hand plunged right through the perfect, flowered wallpaper, and she was horrified to see, spilling from the ensuing hole, a flood of carpenter ants and sawdust. The beautiful wallpaper was hiding an invasion of varmints that had managed to eat away most of the wood before their discovery, resulting in the need for extensive foundational repairs.

This is what it's like when a Christian's life lacks virtue.

Christians Aren't Perfect

Virtue should be an easy topic among believers, but more and more, it's a sore spot. Virtue is essentially moral behavior; it means conducting one's self in line with a moral code. Choosing to do what is right as opposed to what is wrong. A life marked by moral excellence.

Yes, Christians don't become perfect people when they accept Jesus. Yes, even when we fall into sin, God loves us unconditionally, covers us with grace, and redeems us through Christ. Yes, he forgives. Yes. Yes. Yes.

Still, Christ calls us to excellence. He died for our sins, but he doesn't desire that we abuse his grace or disparage his sacrifice by disregarding his command to live according to his Word. We're freed not only from sin but also from choosing to sin.

Why virtue has become a source of debate in the church is baffling (except we know it has to do with false teaching and a twisting of the good by dark forces). As challenging as it is to make right choices when surrounded by wrong ones, life is clearly worse when people choose what is wrong.

And have you noticed the world is entirely two-faced about moral behavior in Christians? They scorn believers who live according to morally sound choices but write derisive headlines for Christians who fall short of ethical standards.

Honoring Excellence in Virtue

The world honors excellence in other areas. We host Olympics to highlight athletic excellence. We bestow degrees to honor academic excellence. There are awards for excellence in the arts and medals for military conduct. We even honor compassionate excellence through humanitarian recognition. Yet all the while, moral excellence has become something suspect, something unachievable, something mocked on late-night television. While we expect the world to be conflicted about virtue, Christians shouldn't be.

In 2 Peter 1:5, the apostle mentions virtue immediately after faith, and I believe the immediacy is no accident. Once we enter into relationship with Jesus by faith, having received forgiveness for our sins and freedom from slavery to sin, our next question should be, *How then should we live going forward?* Peter and Paul warn that, while we are free, our freedom isn't a license to misbehave. First Peter 2:16 says: "Live as people who are free, not using your freedom as a cover-up for evil, but living as servants of God." Galatians 5:13 says: "You were called to freedom, brothers and sisters; only don't let this freedom be an opportunity to indulge your selfish impulses, but serve each other through love" (ESV).

None of us sets out to live lives like my friend's living room—lovely on the outside but corrupt beneath the surface. Just as the ants nibbled the wood, so do small immoral actions mount over time and destroy the framework of our witness for Christ this side of glory.

Unlike the Olympics, moral excellence is no competition. It's dangerous to compare one person's goodness with another's. God says we all have sinned and fall short. We all stand in need of Jesus at all times. We don't seek to have virtue in increasing measure so we can be the most moral person in our small group. We do it so we'll be effective and fruitful in our knowledge of Jesus Christ.

As we spend time exploring what God's Word has to say about virtue and moral excellence, keep the following verses handy lest you forget about his forgiveness and grace:

- If we confess our sins, he is faithful and just to forgive us our sins and cleanse us from everything we've done wrong. (1 John 1:9)
- All have sinned and fall short of God's glory, but all are treated as righteous freely by his grace because of a ransom that was paid by Christ Jesus. (Romans 3:23-24)
- Now there isn't any condemnation for those who are in Christ Jesus. (Romans 8:1)

Word Study Exercise

The specific word Peter uses for virtue (*arete*[1]) appears twice in 2 Peter 1:3, 5. Peter uses it also in 1 Peter 2:9, which most versions translate as "praises" or "excellencies," and it's the word Paul uses in Philippians 4:8. List some moral behaviors or attitudes that most people consider excellent or praiseworthy.

Next, read the following passages and list the behaviors these biblical writers say should be exemplary of Jesus followers:

Romans 12
1 Corinthians 6
1 Corinthians 10:23-33
2 Corinthians 6
Galatians 5
Ephesians 4:17–5:21
Philippians 2
Colossians 3:1-17
1 Thessalonians 4:1-12
2 Thessalonians 3:6-13
Hebrews 13
James 1:19-27

1 Peter 1:13-17
1 John 4:7-21

What effect would it have on your local community if all the believers who lived there behaved according to these passages? What would it mean to you to live surrounded by Christians who displayed these excellent behaviors?

How can we encourage one another to have the quality of virtue in increasing measure? What's the difference between the images these verses bring to mind and the way modern media characterize "virtuous" people?

Does it make any sense that a person growing in these characteristics would be boring, stiff, humorless, arrogant, judgmental, or hypocritical? In what ways do we allow the media to influence our attitudes about our own faith? How do we let the media play the role of Jack's mother (in the beanstalk story) in our lives, and what would be different if we stopped?

Biblical Role Model Ministudy

Read the story of Joseph in Genesis 37, 39–46. List the ways in which others wronged Joseph.

How did Joseph respond to these wrongs?

How did Joseph respond to temptation and trial?

How does it appear Joseph responded to power and riches?

Read 2 Chronicles 16:9, Proverbs 15:3, Luke 16:10, Hebrews 12:1-3, and Genesis 39:23. What do these verses tell us about the value of making right choices even when wronged, even when it feels as though no one is watching?

Choose one of these biblical figures known for making excellent choices in trying times to study deeper: Ruth, Esther, Daniel, Mary, or Joseph, the father of Jesus.

When they made the right choices, was the likely outcome clear?

What pressures were on them when they had to make virtuous choices? Were people around them making choices informed by virtue? What resulted from their choices for them, for people around them, for the kingdom of God?

What lesson do you learn from these people's lives?

Heritage of Faith Walkers

How does virtue manifest itself in our lives? How do virtuous people respond to God, to challenges, to opposition, to disappointments, and to blessings? One wonderful example of virtuous living is Corrie ten Boom (1892–1983), a Dutch Christian who, along with her family, hid Jews during World War II. She was eventually arrested and imprisoned at Ravensbruck concentration camp, where her sister, Betsie, died. Corrie's bestselling book about the experience, *The Hiding Place,* became a 1975 movie.

Other names that come to mind are Billy Graham, Luis Palau, Beth Moore, Christine Caine, and Dietrich Bonhoeffer. Choose one who inspires you and look at the virtuous or excellent practices they incorporate into their daily lives. Cultivate at least one of those practices in your life. Chat with a person from your faith community who exemplifies virtue. What counsel or encouragement does he or she have for you about growing in virtue?

Small Steps Toward Slaying Giants

1. Choose one of the passages you just studied and read it every day this week. Ask God to show you what that verse looks like applied in your life right now. Record his answer and then put it into practice.
2. How has this study inspired you (or reminded you) to think differently about virtue or excellent behavior? If God has shown you areas requiring repentance or growth, what is your plan to follow through with what needs to change? Remember to rely on the power of the Holy Spirit when making behavior changes. Change is a process. Seek God's help, keep the verses on grace handy, and invite a believing friend to support you.

One Stone for Your Sling: Just as the ants nibbled the wood, so do small, immoral actions mount over time and destroy the framework of our witness for Christ this side of glory.

Virtue

Day Two

I Want You to Think About Uriah the Hittite

Virtue That Protects

I was thinking about Uriah the Hittite.

Specifically I was thinking about the moments right before his death—moments when a smart, seasoned soldier might suddenly realize his king had set him up to die.

God recorded Uriah's story in 2 Samuel 11. We usually aim the spotlight on King David in this story because he's our hero. This chapter in Samuel isn't the end of David's story. He falls here—falls far—but he rises through God's redemptive love.

It is, however, the end of Uriah's story. (At least the part of his story that we'll know this side of glory.) That's the point I was thinking about. How Uriah's story ends.

Uriah's actions were those of a man with a soldier's honor. He was a warrior for Israel. He was one of David's mighty men (2 Samuel 23:8-39). He was seasoned. He'd been around. When his king called him from the front lines and indulged him with rich food and wine, Uriah must have been flattered, but it's likely he remained on guard. This wasn't protocol.

After the evening's revelry, rather than enjoy the comfort of his wife, Bathsheba, Uriah camped out with David's servants. Since his comrades-in-arms wouldn't enjoy comforts that night, he reasoned, why should he? He was in the middle of a war; it was no time to go soft. He'd conditioned himself to go without many things during seasons of battle.

Or perhaps he knew the king had slept with his woman. Servants tell tales. Word travels. Uriah was no fool.

Maybe he was subtly reminding David that a king shouldn't sit behind castle walls while his army battled. David had misplaced his loyalty, but Uriah hadn't.

With this choice, Uriah foiled David's attempt at a cover-up. Had Uriah simply spent one night with his wife, the child she carried might have been mistaken as his. No one else would ever know it was David's offspring.

If Uriah suspected he'd outsmarted David, he had to know only danger lay ahead. His king, his leader, his hero was choosing to take them all down a dark, dark path.

David then handed Uriah a letter for Joab, the head of David's army. It contained David's murderous instructions. Uriah carried the orders for his own death sentence. That was how trustworthy he was! David had full confidence that Uriah wouldn't open the letter.

At the king's instruction, Joab sent his friend, his comrade-in-arms, one of David's heroes, to the front line. He implemented a strategy known for its high rate of failure against such cities. Uriah had to have seen the folly of it, but he followed orders.

Then, when the battle was at its thickest, Uriah's fellow warriors pulled back. That moment inspired this chapter. That precious moment when Uriah saw his friends fall away, withdraw, leave him without help against the enemy.

Did he retrace the last hours in his mind? Did the pieces fall into place like a gallows puzzle? Did he look at the other fighters who died before him, knowing those men perished not for the glory of Israel but to camouflage his murder? Perhaps a soldier who displayed such loyalty and honor embraced the death that befell him, knowing those who survived lived in a world in which their king had lost his way.

I don't know what he was thinking, but I know he died because a man who loved God plotted to cover up his own furlough into sin. I want you to think about Uriah the Hittite, too, because what happened to Uriah is what results when the people of God abandon their posts.

There is a time for every soldier (Christian) to rest. There is a time for

Sabbath-taking. There is a day, even for warriors, for quiet reflection and retreat. But this story didn't happen when it was time to rest. It happened when it was time to fight.

Second Samuel 11 opens with these words: "In the spring, when kings go off to war, David sent Joab, along with his servants and all the Israelites, and they destroyed the Ammonites, attacking the city of Rabbah. But David remained in Jerusalem."

At the time when kings go off to war, David remained behind. He vacated his post.

There is a subtle whisper in the air during these times, and it lands on weary Christian ears. It sounds something like this: *You've done so much for others. You deserve a break. No one is perfect, so why are you trying to be? Don't you trust God's forgiveness and grace? You can indulge yourself a little. Look at King David. Why, he committed adultery, but God forgave him. Ease up a little. You've been good for so long it would be completely understandable if you went a little crazy for once. Maybe you're being harder on yourself than God wants you to be. Who do you think you are? You're only human. Go ahead. Look at her. She's beautiful, and she can be yours for a night. No one ever has to know.*

The voice often comes just past middle age when we've worked faithfully for years. It's not obvious because we'd catch on to obvious. It's the Trojan horse of temptations because it sounds a little like the wisdom of self-care and appears to come from within our own thoughts.

But it's a killer.

Unfortunately, the victims are usually others. Yes, God's grace is vast and he forgives and redeems, but in the season of our indulgent sin, we leave others at the mercy of the enemy.

This isn't about continuing a particular ministry; it's about maintaining communication with Jesus and a Christlike mind-set. We can resign from chairing the Christian education committee without abandoning the battle. In fact, it's possible for Christian leaders to remain active at their ministries even as they retreat from Christ. It's fine to rest from a particular ministry as long as you don't vacate your relationship with Jesus by venturing into disobedience.

I want you to think about Uriah the Hittite. What happened to Uriah is what results when the people of God abandon their posts.

We're at war, loved ones. Let's unite in making every effort to reduce casualties. Let us spur one another on to love and good deeds. "Let's not get tired of doing good, because in time we'll have a harvest if we don't give up" (Galatians 6:9).

We all get tired. We all endure long, demanding stretches without due credit or reward. When you hear the whisper, *Bathsheba can be yours, and it won't hurt a soul,* I want you to think about Uriah the Hittite.

Small Steps Toward Slaying Giants

1. Read 2 Samuel 11. Make a note at every juncture where David had an opportunity to make a virtuous decision. We often claim we "fell" into sin or were "carried away." Think of times when you've been tempted to sin but resisted. What helped you make excellent choices?
2. God sent the prophet Nathan to David. Read 2 Samuel 12 and Psalm 51. Are there Nathans in your life? Are there people who would be willing to call you out if they saw you making choices that would take you in a bad direction? If yes, thank God for them and send them notes of thanks. If no, ask God to send you a Nathan who could be there for you in moments of weakness, doubt, or temptation.

One Stone for Your Sling: I want you to think about Uriah the Hittite. Not everyone made it out of the David and Bathsheba story alive.

Virtue

Day Three

My Friend Put Ice Cream in Her Toaster

Practical Virtue

Friend: I'm really struggling lately over my toaster. It keeps breaking down.

Me: Is that ice cream inside the toaster?

Friend: Yeah, why? I like to put ice cream in my toaster.

Me: Well, that's why it keeps breaking down. It wasn't designed for ice cream.

Friend: I feel as if you're judging me.

Me: I'm sorry. I just think if you stop putting ice cream in your toaster it will stop breaking down.

Friend: Well, now I feel bad. You're making me feel bad about myself.

Me: You'll probably feel better if you stop putting ice cream in your toaster.

Friend: Hey, it's *my* toaster. I have a right to do anything I want with it. Are you saying I don't?

Me: I don't think so. It's not about your rights. It's about the design of the toaster.

Friend: Now you're an expert on toaster design. How do you know it's bad to put ice cream in a toaster?

Me: I'm not an expert, but you said it does keep breaking down.

Friend: You can't be 100 percent sure it's the ice cream. Doesn't your toaster ever break down?

Me: Well, sometimes it does, but then I check the instructions or get it repaired.

Friend: You think you're superior to me because mine keeps breaking down. What do you do with your toaster?

Me: I use it to make toast.

Friend: That sounds very old-fashioned and restrictive. I guess some people don't have a need to be creative or free, but that's not me. I like to color outside the box.

Me: How is that not you judging me?

Friend: I'm not judgmental. I'm just defending myself against your oppression.

Me: I'm oppressing you by suggesting your toaster will function better if you don't put ice cream in it?

Friend: That's right. My father said the same thing. He even thumped the instruction booklet on the counter thinking that would change my mind.

Me: Let me look at the instruction booklet. Ah, here it says not to let the toaster come into contact with liquids.

Friend: Does it specify ice cream? Does it specifically prohibit the use of ice cream?

Me: The ice cream seems pretty liquid right now.

Friend: This feels like legalism to me.

Me: It's not legalism. It's about respecting the design of your toaster.

Friend: Wow. I never would have expected this from you. I don't think we can be friends anymore. I need friends who respect my freedom and my rights.

Me: What if we stop discussing the toaster and agree to disagree?

Friend: Unless you support me in putting ice cream in my toaster, I don't feel safe around you.

Me: Okay, well, I certainly want you to be safe; but you have to know, it isn't safe to put ice cream in a toaster.

Friend: You really have to leave now.

I've had this conversation more than once about a wider range of topics than toasters. How about you?

We seem to be becoming a society of horses and mules. "I will instruct you and teach you about the direction you should go. I'll advise you and keep my eye on you. Don't be like some senseless horse or a mule, whose movement must be controlled with a bit and a bridle. Don't be anything like that!" (Psalm 32:8-9).

Freedom without responsibility or respect for our design is lunacy and, ultimately, not freedom at all. Judging others is wrong, and none of us needs that. But all of us, at one time or another, need correction, instruction, and counsel.

Are you free to put ice cream in your toaster? Sure, knock yourself out. But it's no good for your toaster, and in the end you'll be without a toaster *and* ice cream.

Small Steps Toward Slaying Giants

1. Read Proverbs 8–9. List the benefits promised when we follow wisdom. List the consequences of ignoring it. Look especially at 9:7-9. What is the difference between the ways wise people receive correction and how foolish ones receive it?
2. Read Ezekiel 33:1-9 and James 5:19-20. What do these passages say about our responsibility to speak the truth even if no one listens? Is there a place you've been silent when you should have spoken? Ask God to give you courage to open your mouth at the right time and in the right spirit.

One Stone for Your Sling: It's not about your rights. It's about the design of the toaster.

Virtue

Day Four

Playing the Slots at Casino Church

Virtue for a Purpose

Miracles are cool. Undeniable crowd-pleasers.

I've witnessed miracles, received miracles, and prayed for miracles. I believe in them and look forward to more.

In the church, we love a good miracle story—something church insiders call *testimonies*. They are bona-fide healings, unexpected checks for exactly the lacking amount, and people rescued from rivers or wrecks by first responders whom no one can find after the event. These stories are potatoes and gravy on the Sunday morning circuit.

Recently, though, I was in a group discussion with a writer trying to spread her story. It's a true tale of obedience that resulted in miracles. "Do I lead," she asked, "with the obedience or the miracles?"

Spectacular question.

Seems as though the most spiritual answer is to say obedience is the headliner. Right? But we know our fellow humans. Who's going to show up for a talk on obedience? Better to lead with the miracles, sure to draw a crowd, then slip them the real message like slivers of carrot hidden inside a tasty cake.

Tough call. I won't tell you where the group of writers came down on this. I'd like you to weigh in.

Me? I waver.

The message of Christ is obedience. In John 14:15, he says, "If you love me, you will keep my commandments." Simple, straight-up Jesus. Love results in obedience.

Still, God didn't shy away from miracles. Right out of the gate, he led off

Jesus's arrival with a pregnant virgin, angelic visitations, dreams, and water turned into fine wine. He designed us. He knows what gets our attention.

One comment during the discussion with the writer left me thinking, though. Someone said her tagline should be "Obedience results in miracles." I do believe it does and it did in her case, but I don't believe it always does.

The Gospel records, in John 6, a discussion Jesus had with the crowds after he'd performed the miracle of the loaves and fishes and left the area. They followed him, and he chided them for seeking him only for the bread. He then pointed them to the bread they should be looking for—the Bread of Life.

When we're children, we sometimes have to have our vegetables disguised and hidden inside cake, but as we grow, we learn the value of developing an appetite for unadorned broccoli. There are times in all of our lives when miracles are in order, but our appetite should be for Jesus and expressing our love for him through obedience. This healthy appetite will get us through the times when obedience does not, in fact, result in a miracle.

Those times will come.

Daniel's three friends who were thrown into the fiery furnace proclaimed this truth: "If our God—the one we serve—is able to rescue us from the furnace of flaming fire and from your power, Your Majesty, then let him rescue us. But if he doesn't, know this for certain, Your Majesty: we will never serve your gods or worship the gold statue you've set up" (Daniel 3:17-18).

But if he doesn't... These are the words to tattoo on the forearm of your soul. Obedience isn't the quarter we slip into God's slot machine when hoping for a payoff in golden miracles. Obedience is the outward expression of our love for Jesus. Every time we obey, our actions say, "Yes, you are worthy. Yes, Jesus, you are what I seek more than health, more than money, more than a spectacular testimony. My appetite is not for miracles. I hunger for you."

Why is this important to understand? Because when our obedience doesn't result in a miracle, Satan slithers up beside us, whispering lies: *Your obedience was worthless. He didn't even notice. It wasn't enough. You aren't good enough. He isn't a good God. He's unfair. He's withholding something from you. You should get it yourself.*

We need to be equipped then, prepared to access the understanding that comes from God's Word. Obedience isn't the coin of God's realm. We're not in a casino church. God may send a miracle, *but even if he doesn't,* we will not serve any other god.

God supplies miracles when miracles are called for, but obedience is our way of showing our love to Christ. People who obey often witness miracles, but that's because people who obey are more likely to be where God is at work.

Should my writer friend lead with obedience or miracles? What headlines in your life? How have you responded when your obedience has not resulted in a miracle? Let others hear those stories, loved one.

Small Steps Toward Slaying Giants

1. Have you been waiting for a miracle that seems slow in coming? Is it wearing away at your patience, your faith, or your desire to continue to obey? God sees your struggle and wants to strengthen you in it. Read 2 Chronicles 16:9. Talk to God and tell him about your discouragement and your need for strength. Trust that his eyes are on you even if your miracle hasn't come. Seek him more than you seek the miracle, and rest in his sovereignty and grace.
2. Read Hebrews 11:32-40. What does this passage tell us about the outcome of our faith in this life?

❧ ❧ ❧

One Stone for Your Sling: People who obey often witness miracles, but that's because people who obey are more likely to be where God is at work.

Virtue

Day Five

Jurassic Jesus

Powerful Virtue

Have dinosaurs ever taught you a lesson about Jesus?

When I left the movie theater after watching *Jurassic World*, my daughter asked why I kept glancing from one side of the parking lot to the other. Sheepishly, I had to admit I was keeping an eye out for velociraptors.

Okay, I truly escaped into the flick, and my emotions took time to reengage with reality. Eventually I calmed down, but later in the week, I experienced the same sort of nervous jumpiness. It was while I was reading one of the Gospels.

That's right. Jesus made me as nervous as a velociraptor.

If we learn anything from the *Jurassic Park* franchise of movies, it's that the people who live are the ones who respect the risk involved with dinosaurs, appreciate their wildness, and don't try to exploit them, tame them, or use them as weapons of mass destruction. All other people die. Additionally, in the latest Jurassic offering we learn attempts to manufacture replicas have consequences as well.

Even though I'm no paleontologist or geneticist, I can relate to this because people constantly try to treat Jesus as if he's tame, domesticated, toothless, and controllable. They try to create a new Jesus by combining their favorite qualities and eliminating the ones they don't like. I keep looking for that Jesus in the Bible, but I just don't find him.

Frankly, Jesus wasn't always nice. Yes, he drew crowds. Yes, he was welcome at sinners' dinner tables. But I think people stop reading at the ends of these little stories and skip the passages where Jesus said hard things that made crowds walk away. They neglect the impact of passages that tell of Jesus going after religious authorities with colorful analogies. They clearly don't read where he sharply corrected even those in his inner circle, challenged them, warned them, and challenged them again.

The hero of *Jurassic World,* Owen Grady, worked well with dinosaurs because he respected their nature. He invested time with them, established a bond, and always remembered he didn't own them. Alternately, the villainous Hoskins, the security chief with a deadly secret, saw them as potential weapons and orchestrated a dinosaur DNA upgrade that eventually bit him in the... Well, you'll have to see the movie to find out.

We sometimes do that with Jesus. We want him to function as the weapon against our enemies. We want to train him to do tricks and miracles at our  command. We decide to disassemble Jesus, to try to take parts of him and parts of other religious philosophies to create our own version of a god—Jesus 2.0. Then we wonder why we feel as if we're running for our lives.

Jesus is God incarnate. God in the flesh. The God on Mount Sinai, the God who destroyed Sodom and Gomorrah, the God who drowned Pharaoh's armies. This same God told parables, healed the sick, and welcomed the children. God is the same yesterday, today, and tomorrow.

God is greater than we are. We're his creation. He wants to be known, but he's not interested in being re-created, updated, or made more relevant for a new generation. He has revealed himself as he wants to be known. When we invest time knowing him, building a relationship, and reminding ourselves that, yes, we're his friends but always he is the Lord Almighty, then we live. In fact, we live amazing, thrilling, adventurous lives.

Alternately, those who decide they can master Jesus, put him on a leash, and train him to perform tricks on command will find they're mistaken. At heart we know this, don't we?

John 8 contains a fascinating discussion that Jesus had with the crowd. He was direct. He stated his position clearly. At the end, they picked up stones to throw at his head.

This is Jesus. A man who made people want to kill him. In fact, that's what eventually happened. A crowd cried out for his crucifixion. They were incited by the religious leaders of the day, but why? If Jesus was such a nice guy, if Jesus didn't expect that people change, if Jesus brought a message that everyone is all right, then why plot his destruction? Yes, he was welcome at parties, but if all he did was tell entertaining stories, how did he wind up on the cross?

Jesus was dangerous. He stated dangerous truths. The powers of the day saw this. They tried to find ways to control him, and when they couldn't, they killed him. The brilliant news for us is that he didn't stay dead. That fact alone should convince people we're not dealing with a power we can control.

Jesus is the most dynamic, exciting, creative, exhilarating, fascinating, loving, holy, forgiving, frightening, powerful, life-giving force in existence. He's worth knowing, but he didn't come to adorn bumper stickers and T-shirts. He didn't come to be the mascot for a cause. He didn't come solely to make people feel good about themselves.

He came to give us life. He is a force. Have you met Jurassic Jesus?

Tomorrow, when you open your Bible, read one of the Gospels until you feel nervous, as if you'll spend the day on the lookout for velociraptors. Who knows, you might get a glimpse of Jesus.

Small Steps Toward Slaying Giants

1. How do people in your community, family, workplace, school, or other sphere of influence describe Jesus? Where do they get their ideas or information about Jesus? Have you ever asked them? How about you? How do you describe Jesus? Where do you get most of your ideas about what he was like? Have people ever had a wrong idea about you? Where do you want people to get their idea of you?

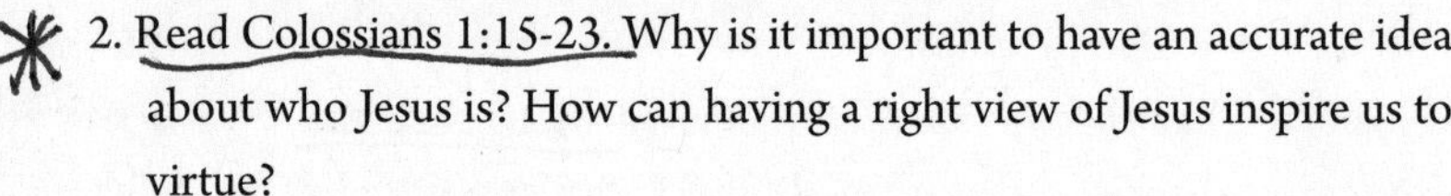

2. Read Colossians 1:15-23. Why is it important to have an accurate idea about who Jesus is? How can having a right view of Jesus inspire us to virtue?

One Stone for Your Sling: Jesus was dangerous. He stated dangerous truths. The powers of the day saw this. They tried to find ways to control him, and when they couldn't, they killed him.

Virtue

Day 6

Pray, Reflect, Process, Pray

Ask God to direct you to activities that will give you virtue in increasing measure. One activity that frequently inspires us to increasing virtue is serving others. Visit one of the elderly from your faith community, help a single parent with yard work or childcare, or donate time to the local homeless shelter. These activities don't make us virtuous, but they do remind us of the intrinsic reward of doing what is right.

Reflect on what you've read in his Word this week. Go back to passages that spoke to where you are right now or inspired you to growth. Reread and reflect.

Everyone processes differently. Some do their best thinking while engaging in physical activities. Others process through creative means. Still others process best by talking things through with someone else. Reflect on your chosen Bible passage, then engage in your preferred activity with the intent of processing what God has said to you through it about virtue.

When you're done, ask God to continue the work of building your virtue in increasing measure.

Now, lather, rinse, repeat. In other words, if this works for you, do it with other passages on virtue or sections of the book that spoke to you.

11

Knowledge for the Climb

Knowledge

Day One

No one likes a know-it-all.

Yet we all enjoy watching know-it-alls learn that they don't know it all.

My friend knew everything about raising children. He liked to share his wisdom with those of us who were actually doing it. Many of our choices were clearly wrong, and he knew why. He had education, books, studies, and articles to back his opinions. What he didn't have was children.

It was delicious for us all when they came along. No one had to say a word. We simply sat back and watched his theories shrivel before the flesh-and-blood reality of tiny humans with minds of their own. Our friend had less to say at our gatherings. Whenever he experienced moments of parenting panic, we nudged him gently in the right direction. No need to rub it in.

We all think we know things. I knew a lot when I was fresh out of college with my shiny degrees in psychology and biblical studies. I'd earned high grades in all my courses and the praise of my professors. I was confident I knew my stuff.

One of my first nights as full-time staff at a runaway shelter in Providence,

Rhode Island, I interviewed a woman while my supervisor observed through the two-way mirror. Two young boys had come to us for shelter, and their mother sat before me to present her understanding of their situation.

As I entered the room, she burst into tears. "I'm a terrible mother," she said. "They were right to run away. I'm awful at parenting."

"No, I'm sure that's not true," I said with great passion, knowing from my schoolwork many parents doubt their own skills. "Don't ever say things like that. I'm sure you're a fine parent."

"You really think so?" she asked, reaching for a tissue.

"Of course," I said with all confidence. I practically quoted from my textbook. "Most parents feel unsure at one time or another. Doubting your instincts can create a completely new set of problems. Like many parents, you have to learn to trust yourself. You know more about parenting than you realize."

She sighed. "I feel much better now. I'll bet you're right! The boys complain about me handcuffing them to their beds at night, but what else am I supposed to do? I need to find a man, and I can't trust the boys on their own, not when I stay out all night. I did worry when there was a fire at the house next door, but it all worked out. The fire never made it to our place. My mom never would have thought of using handcuffs on us. We got into all kinds of trouble when she'd go out all night. I probably am doing better than I realized."

In the lengthy conversation with my supervisor that followed this interview, I learned a couple of things. The first was never to offer assurances without sufficient information, and the second was, even with what I knew, I needed to understand much more to be truly effective in this field. Some knowledge we gain only through experiences like that one, and usually those lessons make the deepest impression.

Unfortunately our culture has taken its distaste for know-it-alls to pathological levels by downplaying the value of knowing things at all. Some would even argue that the few things we say we do know are up for debate.

Rather than esteem them, we relegate people with extensive knowledge to geek status. We refer to them as "brainiacs" or "nerds" and expect them to be socially inept and useless outside their specific area of interest.

The church doesn't do much better in this department. While it's vitally important to put what we know about God and his Word to use, we can't put to use what we don't actually know. We've come a long way from the days when the Bible was studied in public schools. As mentioned earlier, many believe biblical literacy has reached a crisis state. Why is that a big deal? you may ask. Didn't Jesus criticize the Pharisees for being puffed up with their knowledge and not living it out? Isn't it more important to live our faith than to know Bible facts and be good at Bible Jeopardy?

Imagine an athlete trying out for the NFL. He's talented, athletic, and passionate about the game, but he doesn't know any of the rules. Or imagine a musician applying for the Boston Philharmonic. She's mastered music theory, understands everything about the violin including how it's made, and can list every major violin piece ever written, but she's never picked up a violin. One individual has actions without knowledge; the other has knowledge without actions. Both are useless.

There are many barriers to growing in the knowledge of our faith. One of those is that we can become convinced that our only choice is Bible knowledge *or* life application. It is possible to know the Bible and not be arrogant and hypocritical about it. The problem with the Pharisees wasn't their knowledge. The problem was their attitudes, their unwillingness to put into practice what they knew, and their penchant for using what they knew to harm others.

God chose to communicate with us through his written Word and through the person of Jesus Christ. These, and creation, are the key ways he's revealed himself to us. People who love him desire to know him more.

People who love football know everything about the game. My dad played football in high school and is an avid Patriots fan. He knows rules, statistics, plays, coaches, and players. When he played, he practiced for hours and sacrificed to be on the field in order to excel. My friend Heather puts similar passion into her music. People who love music, especially people who play instruments, learn all they can about their favorite genre. They learn the basics of the instruments and practice, but their passion drives them to deepen their knowledge of their craft for as long as they live.

An important way to grow in knowledge of God is through his Word. People who are passionate about knowing God find ways to incorporate it into our lives, don't we? We may get off track sometimes, but we find creative ways to increase in our understanding of this living book. Some follow Bible reading plans. Some use devotionals focusing on themes or short passages. Others attend Bible studies and church classes or pursue formal study. People also memorize Scripture a verse at a time or meditate on a single passage for weeks to gain a better understanding.

I know a busy young man who grew up learning the Bible at home and at church. He's crunched for time right now, so he's focusing on reading one verse a day but working to find ways to live that verse through the day. He copies it from his phone's Bible app to an electronic notepad and reminds himself of it through the day. I am in my car a lot for work, so I listen to the Bible on CD and play songs based on Bible verses. I'm terrible at memorization, so songs help me keep words in my mind. Some listen to Bible podcasts while working out or meditate on verses by stitching them on quilt squares.

In oral societies, Bible storytelling is vital, as are testimonies about how to apply it. We can increase in knowledge of God through watching films, hearing sermons, and even looking at Bible picture books or great art. Everyone has a different capacity for reading and learning. I don't believe God holds people with a greater hold on Bible facts in higher esteem than others. What he cares about is that we seek to know him as best we can and live what we know by his grace. The decline in biblical literacy, however, isn't because most of us don't have the capacity. Too often, we let less important pursuits get in the way.

In a 2014 article for *Charisma Magazine,* journalist Ed Stetzer summarizes the consequence of this lack of knowledge with these words: "Simply put, we have a biblical literacy deficit in part because we have a spiritual maturity deficit. Plenty of research shows the correlation between spiritual maturity and reading the Bible. If you want spiritually mature Christians, get them reading the Bible. That's a statistical fact, but more importantly, it's a biblical truth."[1]

In the pursuit of spiritual growth, it makes sense we should grow in knowledge.

Word Study Exercise

As I've studied the mention of *knowledge* in Scripture, I've realized it's not generally a stand-alone quality. Read the following passages and list the purpose, the result, the priority, or the channel for knowledge mentioned in the verses:

Luke 1:76-79
Romans 11:33-36
Romans 15:14
1 Corinthians 1:4-5
1 Corinthians 13
2 Corinthians 2:14-17
2 Corinthians 4:6
2 Corinthians 6:3-10
2 Corinthians 8:7
2 Corinthians 10:4-6
Ephesians 3:14-21
Philippians 3:8
Colossians 2:1-3
2 Peter 3:18

You will have noted that while love is greater than knowledge, knowledge is still elevated as a priority. Those without a biblical worldview make knowledge and love either/or propositions, but in Christ, they work together to grow us up to full maturity.

Consider what you have noted about knowledge as you read these verses. What step will you take to grow in your knowledge of Jesus in the month to come?

Biblical Role Model Ministudy

Paul was an intelligent, educated, respected Jewish citizen of Rome when he entered into relationship with Jesus Christ. His knowledge of Jesus didn't puff him up; instead, he became a servant of the church he had once persecuted. Read Acts 15. How did Paul's, Barnabas's, Judas's, and Silas's knowledge serve to strengthen and unite the body of Christ?

Heritage of Faith Walkers

List Christians whom you admire from history or from your own life and who are examples to you of knowledge. How does knowledge manifest ifself in their lives? How do they respond to God, to challenges, to opposition, to disappointments, to blessings?

Ravi Zacharias, born in 1946, is an Indian-born, Canadian-American apologist, speaker, and author of over twenty books defending the faith. He is a modern example of a person using his knowledge to serve the building of God's kingdom. Others are Lee Strobel, C. S. Lewis, Holly Ordway, Nancy Pearcey, and G. K. Chesterton, to name a few. Choose one who particularly inspires you and look at the knowledge practices he or she incorporated into daily life. Incorporate at least one of those into yours. Invite a biblically knowledgeable person from your faith community to talk to your small group about passion for God's Word and his or her daily Bible study and application habits.

Remember: increasing in knowledge of God isn't about intellectual capacity. People's intelligence and learning abilities vary. Not everyone is a theologian or scholar. God simply calls us to know him, understand his Word the best we're able, and obey what we know. The limitations of our intellectual functioning don't limit God's work in us or through us.

Small Steps Toward Slaying Giants

1. Think about someone you know very well—a parent, sibling, spouse, or close friend. How hard would it be for others to make you doubt that person or convince you of something contrary to your experience of him or her? How then can it help Christians slay the giants of doubt and false teaching to grow increasingly in their knowledge of Jesus?
2. It will be tempting for some, after studying this section, to make ambitious plans for reading through the Bible or studying God's Word throughout the day. There's nothing wrong with that desire, but expansive intentions can easily crumble in the demands of daily life. What is one thing you can do this week to increase your time in God's Word? Start there.

One Stone for Your Sling: People who love Jesus desire to know him more.

Knowledge

Day Two

Why Stuff Happens

Freeing Knowledge

I've done things I regret.

Haven't you? I'm always curious when I meet someone who purports to have no regrets. Especially when that someone made choices that hurt others.

It happened once in a casual public setting, an innocent conversation in a coffee shop. I ran into a local church leader whose actions had disappointed many people, including me. We'd done what we could to work out our peace back at the point of the initial incident. I'd certainly worked to extend forgiveness, knowing how much God has forgiven me, but the coffee shop banter resurrected some old hurts.

The question was posed: "Do you have any regrets?" I focused on my book and sipped my black coffee. The leader briefly acknowledged me as he walked toward the counter.

"Regrets?" He laughed. "Nah, I don't waste time on regrets. Everything happens for a reason. Sure, I've made some mistakes—everyone has—but all those mistakes made me the person I am today. I like who I am. What would I possibly change?"

Faces came to mind. Faces of those he had hurt. But hey, he likes himself now, so it's all good, right?

As I watched him walk from the shop, I asked God to help me forgive again. I thanked God for forgiving me. How often had I shrugged off my poor choices without truly considering the impact they'd had on those around me? God offers his grace freely, but was I guilty of taking it for granted? I thought about how casually we say things without considering what we really mean.

Everything does happen for a reason, but sometimes that reason is sin and evil's reign in parts of this world and in some of us. Christians and others mistakenly distort Romans 8:28: "We know that God works all things together for good for the ones who love God, for those who are called according to his purpose."

Post hoc ergo propter hoc. Translation? "After this, therefore, because of this." This Latin saying is frequently used to refer to the fallacy that because something came before, it caused the thing that came after. That God works good from all things in the lives of those who love him does not mean all things are good.

If a drunk driver kills someone I love and the Lord uses the testimony from that to bring others to Christ, it doesn't retroactively make the drunk driver's choice a good one. If a terrorist group attempts to exterminate an entire people and because of it, the gospel spreads in that region and many come to Christ, it does not ordain terrorism as a method of evangelism.

If I lie and gossip (which I have) and people are damaged by my words, but through the process of growing in Christ, I repent; when I write the lesson I learned into a blog post that changes many lives, it doesn't mean my lies and gossip were "meant to be." My lies and gossip happened for a reason—because I chose to sin rather than to access the power of Christ not to sin. God has forgiven my lying and my gossip in the name of Jesus, but I do regret the times I've gossiped or lied and have made amends where I could with those I hurt.

God doesn't bless my bad choices; he redeems them. There's a difference, an important one. Jesus died to pay the price for my sins and to free us from the power of sin. I've mentioned it earlier, but it bears repeating that his death freed us *from* sin, not *to* sin.

Too many of us still cling to the guilt of past sin. That's not God's plan for us. We receive forgiveness and move forward in Christ—free. Yet we always should remember our freedom came at a price—a price paid by someone else, that is, Jesus.

Regrets don't cripple me, but I certainly have them. I don't wish for the church leader from the coffee shop to saddle himself with regret. But the knowledge that past sins have had long-ranging consequences in our lives and in the lives of others can remind us to access the power of Christ to avoid sin going forward. The fact that Jesus carries the weight of our sin, in many ways, frees us to own up to it in ways we couldn't bear on our own. We can acknowledge the damage resulting from our poor choices, knowing Jesus has the power to transform and will give us the strength to repair relationships where we can.

The cross is not a cover-up or whitewash of the nature or severity of our crimes. Jesus didn't pretend our sins didn't happen or minimize them as "no big deal." He paid the price for them himself. The cross is a signpost of the enormity of sin, and its shadow falls on us all. I have regrets; the cross testifies to that. But it also testifies to the truth that my regrets don't need to own me, because Jesus Christ does.

That is freedom without hiding. Freedom without selective memory. Freedom without revisionist history. When Jesus works all things together for good for those who love him, the point is God's amazing power to redeem and to transform. It amazes precisely because the sinful choices made in this world have such far-reaching power. God's power to overcome is that much greater.

Imagine the healing that could happen in the body of Christ if, instead of dodging our past sins, we said to one another, "I want to tell you I know my choice to sin in that situation caused you harm. I've received forgiveness from Christ, but I'd like to know if there's any way I can make amends to help you heal. And please know I've taken these steps to hopefully make better choices in the future."

Regrets? I have them, but I've given Jesus my regrets, along with everything else in my life, to watch him work good from even my failings.

Small Steps Toward Slaying Giants

1. Many of us have had a distorted understanding of Romans 8:28. It's easy for people (including me) to misunderstand a single verse or to take it out of context. It increases understanding to read the verses around a particular passage and to read other passages of the Bible on similar topics. What are other ways that we can be sure we have a clear understanding of biblical passages?
2. Are there verses you've heard incorrectly applied? What was the effect of that incorrect application? What about sayings attributed to the Bible that aren't actually Scripture, such as "God helps those who help themselves"? What are some loving, kind ways we can correct these types of errors when we hear them?

One Stone for Your Sling: I have regrets; the cross testifies to that. But it also testifies to the truth that my regrets don't need to own me, because Jesus Christ does.

Knowledge

Day Three

Stop Praying! You'll Never Get It Right

Knowledge Applied in Battle

There are spiritual forces at work to discourage you from connecting with God. Often they sound like this: *You should stop praying. He's clearly not listening, or if he is, he's not answering. You're boring him as much as you're boring yourself. If he hasn't answered by now, he isn't going to answer. Stop wasting your breath. Give up.*

"Jesus was telling [the disciples] a parable about their need to pray continuously and not to be discouraged" (Luke 18:1).

He's annoyed with your yammering when you should know what to do already. He's not going to answer because you should know the answer. Why do you keep bothering God with petty things or problems you ought to be able to solve on your own?

"Anyone who needs wisdom should ask God, whose very nature is to give to everyone without a second thought, without keeping score" (James 1:5).

It's because your prayers are selfish, you know. Other people get their prayers answered because they're better than you are. They pray with pure motives. Not you. He sees right through you. Stop praying until you're a better Christian.

"He didn't spare his own Son but gave him up for us all. Won't he also freely give us all things with him?" (Romans 8:32).

It's because you're overweight and out of shape. He's embarrassed by your gluttony and laziness. He won't answer your prayers because you're indulging your sin. Or it's because you spend so much time tending to your own appearance and staying fit. Everyone sees how in shape you are, and you love the attention. He can see through that. He knows you're actually vain and full of sin. That's why he won't listen to your prayers.

"Who will bring a charge against God's elect people? It is God who acquits them. Who is going to convict them? It is Christ Jesus who died, even more, who was raised, and who also is at God's right side. It is Christ Jesus who also pleads our case for us" (Romans 8:33-34).

It's because of that wrong decision you made twenty years back to pursue a degree in business instead of ministry. You were only thinking of yourself. Or it's because of that wrong decision you made twenty years back to enter ministry instead of business. You've always been a glory thief. If only you could go back…

"It's not that I have already reached this goal or have already been perfected, but I pursue it, so that I may grab hold of it because Christ grabbed hold of me for just this purpose. Brothers and sisters, I myself don't think I've reached it, but I do this one thing: I forget about the things behind me and reach out for the things ahead of me. The goal I pursue is the prize of God's upward call in Christ Jesus" (Philippians 3:12-14).

It's because you had sex before marriage. Because your daughter divorced her husband. Because your son's an addict. Because you had lustful thoughts about that coworker. Because you took a year off from serving at church. Because you're too busy in ministry, you've left no room for God. Because you've slacked off at work. Because you're overworking. Because you're an indulgent mother. Because you're too hard on your kids. He's not listening. You should really stop praying until you've cleaned up your act.

"There isn't any condemnation for those who are in Christ Jesus" (Romans 8:1).

Don't you wonder why other people get miracles and not you? You're lacking in faith. He has favorites, and you're not one of them. Those are coincidences. Miracles don't happen anymore. You need to be your own miracle. You're always looking for the easy way out. Stop praying and start working toward what you want.

"The boy's father cried out, 'I have faith; help my lack of faith!'" (Mark 9:24).

You heard how that woman prayed. She's articulate. She started with praise. She always starts with praise. Did you start with praise, or did you jump right in asking for stuff? Didn't you hear that guy pray? God always answers his prayers. He uses a formula. Don't you remember he taught it once? You forgot part of it, didn't you? You need that formula. Confession. Remember that sermon on confessing? Have you confessed everything? That's not even possible, is it? Your sins are endless. You must have missed something. You should stop praying and take stock.

"The Spirit comes to help our weakness. We don't know what we should pray, but the Spirit himself pleads our case with unexpressed groans" (Romans 8:26).

He's not there. Your words aren't getting past the sound of your own voice. Why are you fooling yourself when the evidence is clear that God does not exist? Or if he does, he doesn't care about you.

"Ever since the creation of the world, God's invisible qualities—God's eternal power and divine nature—have been clearly seen, because they are understood through the things God has made" (Romans 1:20).

"I'm convinced that nothing can separate us from God's love in Christ Jesus our Lord: not death or life, not angels or rulers, not present things or future things, not powers or height or depth, or any other thing that is created" (Romans 8:38-39).

Stop praying. You'll never get it right. Go read about prayer. Study more about prayer. Talk with someone about prayer. Listen to a podcast about prayer. Read a prayer blog. Start a prayer journal. Find a prayer partner. Plan a prayer retreat. Do anything except pray.

"Rejoice always. Pray continually. Give thanks in every situation because this is God's will for you in Christ Jesus" (1 Thessalonians 5:16-18).

I've heard the voice, the whisper, the serpent's most toxic weapon, the lies. Nevertheless, I have access, as do you, to the weapon of choice of Jesus Christ, the weapon that stood him in good stead in the moment, the sword of the Spirit, the Word of God. Are you under attack? Pick up the sword, loved one.

Small Steps Toward Slaying Giants

1. Memorized Bible passages are always at our disposal, ready to defend us when the enemy attacks. Romans 8 is a rich passage; there are others. I'm terrible at memorizing, but I know most of Romans 8 well enough to call it to mind when I need it. How about you?
2. Matthew 4:1-11 is the record of Jesus's temptation in the wilderness. Notice that his defense against the evil one is God's Word. What temptations are you facing? Have one or two verses ready to read or speak aloud when temptation comes.

One Stone for Your Sling: We have access to the weapon of choice of Jesus Christ, the weapon that stood him in good stead in the moment, the sword of the Spirit, the Word of God.

Knowledge

Day Four

Battling Bible Boredom

Adventurous Knowledge

Sometimes the Bible bores me.

Yes, I said it. Since we're being honest in this book, I must confess there are times when I open God's Word and get absolutely nothing out of it. Nada. Zilch. Zippo. Nix. No—thing. That used to make me panic. It's God's holy Word, after all. How on earth can it be boring?

That's the key phrase, though, isn't it: "How on earth?" Context is everything. Have you ever told a hilarious story to one group only to find that it falls flat with another? Or have you ever found a book or movie meaningful at one stage of life only to revisit it later and wonder what affected you the first time around? I've no doubt when I'm enjoying eternity there will be no boredom, but on this side of the end times, boredom creeps in like mustard gas and can pave the way for the enemy's favorite weapon—discouragement.

I'm a lover of God's Word. What's not to love about a book full of communication from the Creator of all life? As literature alone it's mesmerizing in its scope, poetry, wisdom, history, prophecy, and uniqueness. It is a miracle of cohesion between inspired human writers spanning thousands of years to produce a singularly unified work. Beyond that, there is power in this book—the power of the living God to convert, to change, to transform, to heal, to counsel, to train, to correct, and to guide.

Since I was a child, I've devoured its pages, knowing the biblical writers and characters better than I know my best friends. Still, on a regular basis, I can read a passage as familiar as Genesis 1 and find some new understanding that deepens my awareness of God. Verses I learned as a child take on fresh meaning as I age, experience a new tribulation, or hear the story of another believer exploring faith from a different perspective.

Then some days I get nothing.

Rather than panic, though, I've come to understand boredom can be used for good in the life of a believer if we turn it over to God.

You see, we humans love novelty, don't we? We have a voracious appetite for the new, the trendy, the unheard, the untried. We see it in the church all the time. *Have you heard this new speaker? Read this new writer? Attended this new conference? Prayed this new way of prayer?* We could patch together a lifetime of chasing the next insight, piece of knowledge, or nugget of truth. There's a danger in that, though.

Years ago, I heard a story about a frustrated pastor. He preached week after week, but no one in his congregation seemed to be changing. He took a drastic step and announced he would preach only one truth at a time until people employed that truth in their lives. He started with "Love the Lord your God with all your heart, with all your soul, and with all your strength." "Do this," he exhorted his people. That month, the congregation broke into groups. They studied and discussed what it would look like to live that verse every day. Slowly they learned to live it. Finally, the pastor preached a second message, "Love your neighbor as yourself," and they began the work of learning to live a second verse.

From that story, I realized when I open God's Word and find it boring, dry, or without savor, it's an opportunity to invite God into my reading for a soul-check. I take my boredom to God and ask, "Are there things you've taught me I'm not applying, Lord? Show me. Teach me to seek you more than I seek new insight and understanding."

You see, we're never reading God's Word in order to fill our minds with great thoughts and puff ourselves up with understanding. We're reading it because it's his side of our conversation. Through it, we know him more deeply.

Many of us begin Bible-reading plans with great intentions. Reading God's Word is always a good thing. Knowing him through it, though, requires application: living God's Word and obeying what we know is our calling. Focus less on keeping up with your reading schedule and more on meeting God on those pages. When God wants to tarry in one spot, let's not trudge ahead chasing our sense of accomplishment more than we chase after him.

When we get bored, rather than leaving the boredom out as a tool of the enemy to discourage us, let's bring it to God, praying, "Lord, I want you more than I want a thrilling new understanding. What's the last thing you said, and how can I start living it right now?" I suspect if we start applying what we read as soon as we read it, life and Bible reading will get exciting fast.

Small Steps Toward Slaying Giants

1. What would happen if you had to report at the end of the week on how you applied Sunday's sermon and the Scriptures you read at church, at small group, and in your devotional time? Try it this week. Expect an adventure.
2. What is your response when children or teens express boredom? I've known young people who expressed boredom in the middle of a national forest or an amusement park. It's a sign they aren't open to being present or they're disengaged. When you hear people are bored with the Bible, what's your response? In what loving, honest ways can we encourage one another to engage with God's Word?

❧ ❧ ❧

One Stone for Your Sling: When I open God's Word and find it boring, dry, or without savor, it's an opportunity to invite God into my reading for a soul-check.

Knowledge

Day Five

Why God Loves Empty Prayers

Life-Giving Knowledge

I started praying and it sounded like this: blah, blah, blah, blah.

Okay, if you had been with me, you would have heard this: "Father God, you are holy. You are awesome. You have all power and might. You're worthy of praise. Thank you for all you've given me in life. Thank you for Jesus."

But if you had been sitting with God, you'd have heard what I suspect he heard: blah, blah, blah, blah.

It's not because I was harboring any more sin than usual. It wasn't because I was using the wrong words or starting at the wrong place in my prayer. It's good to praise God, and I don't discount that here. But at that moment in time, while my mouth was uttering words, my heart was empty.

It didn't take long for me to hear the drone of my own soul, and I stopped. I made eye contact with God for the first time in the prayer (don't ask how this is accomplished, but trust that's what happened). All at once, I heard what he was hearing, and I finally spoke words that matched my soul: "You're right, Lord. You got me. Right now, I got nuthin'."

Why was I speaking then? I searched my mind for real words to express what was happening inside at that moment. Nope. Nothing. "You know, I want to be near you, Jesus. I want to connect with you, but I'm empty."

That's when I heard him. *Then bring me that. Bring me your emptiness.*

What? That's crazy, I thought. Yet what choice did I have? I needed him right then. I wanted him. I craved his presence. When a word person is weary, words leave the building—like Elvis, like "That's all she wrote," like gone, baby, gone. Empty was all I had.

God reminded me of the poor widow in the Bible. Creditors were coming to take her children as slaves, so she went to the prophet Elisha and asked for help. All she had left was a jar of oil. Elisha told her to go to her neighbors and get all of their empty jars. Then he said to go into her home, close her door, and begin pouring her oil. She poured until every jar was full. She had enough oil to sell to pay her debts.

No human would invent our God. Who could imagine a God who says, "Get a whole bunch of empty and bring it to me"?

It's not easy to face our own emptiness. Empty is never something good: empty gas tank, bank account, promises, cupboards. Nope. Not good. Imagine being invited to a party and offering to bring an empty bowl or platter. The only table you'd be a welcome guest at with that kind of contribution is the table of the Lord. Still, what other table matters?

I sat with the Lord—empty. I didn't keep talking because that was ridiculous. I prayed this, "Fine. Here I am. I have nothing to bring you. Not even words. Still, I long for you, so I'm not going to budge from you, even though I have nothing. I'm going to sit here with my nothing and you." I sat for a long time. It felt like . . . sitting. Being quiet. Still. It also felt freeing. This was honest. Real. Home. A place I could show up empty and be welcome. God's heart.

When I concluded, I had no grand insight. I didn't feel especially holy. I knew I had been with Jesus—empty—and it had been okay.

Here's the cool part. A couple of days later, a friend posted a note online about the struggle of striving to work toward a God-given dream and feeling frustrated, weary, and confused. In the midst of the online conversation that ensued, I talked about bringing God our emptiness. What I shared was meaningful to many other people in the discussion.

I hadn't seen it when I rose from that time of sitting with him, but I'd arrived empty and I left so full that I had enough to share with my neighbors. What had I done? Seriously—nothing.

I love watching God work. That's what happens when I sit still and quiet down: I get to see him work, and it's beautiful. Are you running on empty? Bring your empty to Jesus. He's waiting.

Small Steps Toward Slaying Giants

1. Read 2 Kings 4:1-7. What do you do when you feel empty? What does that empty feeling do to your prayer life? Your Bible reading? Your church attendance? What would happen if you brought your emptiness to God?
2. Read Psalm 131 and find a quiet place to sit with God for a time. Invite God to sit with you and then be still before him. You may find it restorative in ways you can't even imagine.

❧ ❧ ❧

One Stone for Your Sling: No human would invent our God. Who could imagine a God who says, "Get a whole bunch of empty and bring it to me"?

Knowledge

Day Six

Pray, Reflect, Process, Pray

Ask God to direct you to activities that will give you knowledge in increasing measure. One activity that can break you out of a Bible rut is to read an entire book of the Bible, such as one of the Epistles, in one sitting, or read from a translation other than your usual to see if familiar passages take on a deeper meaning.

Reflect on what you've read in his Word this week. Go back to passages that spoke to where you are right now or inspired you to growth. Reread and reflect.

Everyone processes differently. After you've reflected on your chosen Bible passage, engage in your preferred activity with the intent of processing what God has said to you through it about faith. When you're done, ask God to continue the work of building your knowledge in increasing measure.

Now, lather, rinse, repeat. In other words, if this works for you, do it with other passages on knowledge.

12

Self-Control for Repeat Offenders

Self-Control

Day One

On my back on the wood floor of the karate school, I prayed someone would pull the fire alarm and end our torture. There were twenty-five of us, all candidates for our black belts, training for our physical test. Some were as young as ten; others of us, over forty. We'd already endured a grueling Saturday morning workout followed by two karate classes. We were ready to go home to our showers and beds. The only thing standing between the door and us was a three-minute leg lift.

That doesn't sound very hard, does it? Lie on your back, keep your legs straight, and lift them at a thirty-degree angle to the floor. Now hold for 180 seconds. It should have been cake. Except it wasn't. Several candidates were beyond their limit and kept dropping their heels to the floor before the instructor released us, so we all had to start again. No one could leave until everyone held the position for the allotted time. I admit there were moments I had very mean thoughts about several of the younger candidates, especially when the exercise went on for thirty minutes.

The floor pooled with sweat. The first few times we had to start over, we groaned or glared at the culprit who had dropped. After a while, though, it took all our effort simply to focus. After twenty minutes, I feared we'd be there until Jesus returned. After twenty-five minutes, I prayed for Jesus to return. I no longer believed we were capable of leg lifts. My ab muscles screamed at me to stop. Some of the younger candidates whimpered quietly.

Finally the instructor said we would have one last opportunity to make this happen. If we didn't, we'd have to complete another forty-five-minute class. That must have rallied some deep, internal stamina none of us realized we had because, finally, every one of us found we could hold our legs up for three minutes.

Prior to this experience, I wouldn't have believed I would be able to do repeated leg lifts for thirty minutes. Following it, I wondered how many other things I thought were beyond my capabilities were actually achievable. Suddenly I saw the benefit of self-control and the importance of proper motivation to activate it.

Celebrating Self-Control

Self-control took quite a hit in the sixties and seventies when America was learning to "let it all hang out." It can certainly be overdone and lead to destructive and unpleasant side effects, but increasing in this characteristic is as natural to spiritual growth as it is to child development.

Parents get excited at every sign that their children are learning to do things independently. They hold up their own heads. They stand. They grasp a spoon or cruise around the room clinging onto furniture. When they control their own bodily functions, it's reason for celebration; but our encouragement to self-control doesn't end there.

We encourage children to control their selfishness by sharing, to control their desire for immediate gratification by refraining from tantrums, to control their self-centeredness by entering into polite conversation with others. We don't see these signs of self-control as binding or restrictive but as signs of maturity. Likewise in the church, we can encourage one another to be our better selves—not because we're so in love with looking proper but as an aspect of mature spiritual living.

As young believers, we find that self-control conversations usually revolve around issues of morality, but at the risk of sounding like the emcee of an infomercial, "Wait! There's more!" As I've grown in the Lord, I find the quality of self-control is instrumental in learning to manage my thought life, defend against obsessive worry or fear, and govern my speech and attitudes. Self-control plays a role in sacrificial giving and loving as well as in controlling the commonly targeted sins of lust and gluttony. In other words, self-control is important for more than simply containing our appetites.

Word Study Exercise

Read Acts 24:22-27. How did Felix react to Paul's teaching about self-control? Why are we also prone to react this way when the topic arises?

Read Galatians 5:16-26. Self-control may be intimidating, but how does lack of self-control reveal itself? How can that help us continue to reach for growth in self-control even when it's challenging or when we suffer failures? What does it look like to "live by the Spirit" (v. 25)? What role does the Holy Spirit play in encouraging our efforts at self-control?

I like the phrase Paul uses here in the ESV translation: "Keep in step with the Spirit" (v. 25). I walk at a much healthier pace when I walk with my friend Kathy, who is an experienced and fit walker. I also make healthier and holier choices when I'm with others who are trying to do the same. What does it look like, in your life, to "live by the Spirit" and "keep in step with the Spirit"?

Read Matthew 5:21-30, 2 Corinthians 10:3-6, and James 1:19-27. Consider the qualities we've studied so far and imagine them, not as isolated characteristics but as ingredients contributing to spiritual maturity by enhancing one another. Do we see in these passages how faith, virtue, and knowledge can support self-control?

Biblical Role Model Ministudy

In the Book of Judges, we find one of God's more colorful creations: the impulsive, headstrong Samson. He's a great study in what happens when a man devoted to God lacks self-control. Read Samson's story in Judges 13–16. What were the consequences, for himself and for his people, of Samson's consistent lack of self-control?

In the end, God did use Samson to free the Israelites from the Philistines, but he used him from within bondage. This is a great illustration of the fact that God can still use us even as we display a need for growth in these characteristics. Most of us would prefer that he use us while we enjoy the freedom found in following his ways, don't you think? How does the world look upon self-control, and how has that affected your thinking about it? What are your thoughts on self-control after reading Samson's story?

Heritage of Faith Walkers

List Christians you admire from history or from your own life who are examples to you of self-control. How does self-control manifest itself in their lives? How do they respond to God, to challenges, to opposition, to disappointments, to blessings?

Be encouraged by Susanna Wesley (1669–1742), a Christian mother best known for raising and educating her ten surviving children (having given birth to nineteen) with strong routines, spiritual discipline, and fortitude in the face of adversity. We credit two of her sons, John and Charles Wesley, with founding Methodism. Other people who exemplify self-control include Rev. Phyllis Sortor, Katie Davis, Frederick Douglass, Richard Foster, and Thomas Becket.

Try to spend time with a believer who regularly exercises self-control. How does it play out in that person's daily life? Is it a struggle for him or her? What counsel does he or she have for you to grow in self-control?*

Small Steps Toward Slaying Giants

1. List your feelings, experiences, and fears about self-control. What teaching or examples have shaped those feelings or fears? Self-control

* A note of caution. If you've been harmed or oppressed by legalism or if you struggle with obsessive-compulsive behaviors or behaviors related to an eating disorder, I strongly urge you to invite a spiritual mentor or your counselor into your growth process in the area of self-control.

is a tricky concept for many due to false teaching, harsh role models, or struggles with anxiety or self-esteem. Give your fears and negative experiences to God. Ask him to redeem your concept of self-control and lead you gently in the right direction.

2. Read 1 Corinthians 9:19-27. What is Paul's motivation for exercising self-control? Read Proverbs 25:28. How does this image spur you on to be ever increasing in self-control?

One Stone for Your Sling: In the church, we can encourage one another to be our better selves—not because we're so in love with looking proper but as an aspect of mature spiritual living.

Self-Control

Day Two

Stand Back! This Is a Job for an Old Woman!

Self-Control for the Ages

I don't know if you've noticed, but God doesn't see old* women the way the world does.

The world looks at gray hair, wrinkles, and saggy parts and says, "Whoa, take a load off, Annie. You sit your old bones over in that rocker and rest up for . . . well, you just rest."

Jesus is just as likely to see the same conglomeration of battered bones and liver spots; but instead of shuffling her off to the home, he's after her with an assignment—and no light duty, either. He called Sarah and Elizabeth to give birth to special babies with callings, Deborah to lead the nation of Israel, Noah's wife to survive when all others were doomed, and countless other old women to similar acts of courage and faith.

Neither does he wink at the sin of old women. He knows that just as some women age with light and grace, others age bent, like gnarled tree roots, or tough and leathered, like beef jerky in a freeze. He doesn't excuse their meanness or their vitriol any more than he excuses the blood lust of young men or the foolish gossip of young girls.

When Athaliah set out to destroy her own family in a bid for power, God had her put to death by the sword. When Jezebel faced judgment for persecuting his prophets, God had her thrown out of a window, her body devoured

---

* Now, *old* is a relative term. As life expectancy rises in a culture, so does our concept of old. We don't know the age of many women in the Bible, as the biblical writers weren't inspired to record most of them. Suffice it to say, God takes women's sin as seriously as men's at every age. The women mentioned were old enough to have children and grandchildren.

by dogs. When Sapphira insisted on lying to the apostles to cover the greed she shared with her husband, moments later she lay cold and dead beside him at the will of the Lord. (See 2 Kings 9:30-37; 2 Kings 11:1-16; Acts 5:1-11.)

God knows old women are a force. Something happens to those of us of a certain age. We lose our need to please people. We understand *nice* isn't one of the fruits of the Spirit. We grasp the value of truth, courage, and perseverance. We know, at its core, love is a sinewy muscle, like the heart, that weathers on despite its burdens and the ravages of time. Love is a feisty thing with bulldog teeth and the iron grip of a mother clinging to a child in a gale-force wind.

Old women without God are agents of evil so terrible there should be a Special Forces unit assigned to hunt down godless women over fifty. Old women sold out to Jesus Christ, though, are light sabers in the hand of the Master Jedi, able to lacerate the darkness with razor precision, to slice away bonds of evil freeing those enslaved, and to light the way for those lost so they may emerge from the catacombs of delusion.

I believe God is raising up old women across the planet to contend against the evil one in the battle for souls. He's fostering a spiritual militia of bold, stouthearted, fearless, articulate, compassionate soldiers adorned with crowns of gray and eyes bright with eternal life.

In April of 2014, thousands of Chinese believers formed a human shield to protect their church. One reporter quoted one strong woman, Yang Zhumei, age seventy-four, as saying, "On Thursday evening, several hundred police officers with bulldozers took up positions around the church. I held their hands and said, 'Comrades, don't take down our cross. I can give you my head instead.' She continued, 'Even if they take my head, I can still find happiness with God,' she shouted."[1]

It takes a few decades on this planet, walking every day with Jesus, to trust there is happiness after decapitation. If Yang Zhumei can face down communist soldiers, others of us can stand up and be heard where we are. We can minister to drug addicts, and we can rock crack babies through withdrawal. We can take planes to foreign lands to fight sex trafficking or serve in orphanages or translate God's Word into unknown languages. We can intercede in the night. We can speak out in the day. We can take on schools that threaten to silence our children when they speak about Jesus, and we can inspire lukewarm believers who usually warm pews to rise up and walk.

Old women are a force—for God or evil. We choose now, and we'll answer for our choice when he returns. We'll either face the dogs like Jezebel or birth new life in our twilight years like Sarah or Yang Zhumei. I pray with the psalmist:

> So, even in my old age with gray hair,
> don't abandon me, God!
> Not until I tell generations about your mighty arm,
> tell all who are yet to come about your strength.
>
> (Psalm 71:18)

Are you with me? Sometimes the job of kingdom building calls for a tough old broad, so rise up, and bring along the old men, too. We can be light sabers, all.

Small Steps Toward Slaying Giants

1. Read Psalm 71. What is the psalmist's view of aging? What is the psalmist's view of God? How have you allowed "Jack's mother" to color your perspective on growing older? What is God's perspective on using older people in building his kingdom? Using a Bible dictionary or reference Bible, research the ages of Moses, Caleb, Joshua, Daniel, John, and other biblical heroes when God pressed them into key points of service or into pivotal circumstances. What does that tell you about God's power and plan even into our later years?
2. Are there areas of self-control that become more challenging as we age? What are they? Are there areas that become less challenging? How can we support and encourage one another to continue developing greater self-control into our later years?

One Stone for Your Sling: Sometimes the job of kingdom building calls for a tough old broad.

Self-Control

Day Three

Spinning Out of Control

Keeping Perspective on Self-Control

In the dark of an early February morning, I was in the passenger seat when our car hit a patch of ice and spun out of control. I don't remember much—a sense of horror, a glimpse of guardrail, the name of Jesus. Those are the impressions that remain of the actual crash.

I don't remember my glasses flying off my face or the seatbelt pressing into my legs and chest enough to cause injury or whacking my knee on something (the dashboard?) hard enough to create a bruise.

Horror. Guardrail. Jesus. That's it.

Sharper is the memory of what followed. Pressing pain in my chest. Incredible cold. Shaking. The dark. Swirling snow. My husband calling 911. He says he's fine. Yes, send a rescue.

Men arrive in turnout coats with neon green stripes. They are speaking kind words I try to receive but reject. Hands are placing me on a backboard. I feel panic. There is a confusing pain in my chest. I can't link it to a cause. Not sufficient to merit this sharp, frightening stab.

I feel anger about the crash. Frustration. Indignation at the thought of lost wages and a damaged car. Then the medical technicians place restraints and blocks around my head. I'm claustrophobic. Panic ratchets higher. I can't find my glasses or my phone. Panic and pain are escalating.

Any history of heart problems? No. How is the pain? An eight now, on that bump a ten, back to an eight, on that turn an eleven. I start to lose it. I can't do this. My kids—is Rob telling them I'm fine? I am fine. They should go to school. Go to work. Drive carefully. No, strike that. Everyone stay home. Be safe, completely safe for this one snow day.

My parents. How to avoid stressing them? I'm fine. Don't let this add to your stress. My job. A client scheduled. I'm not that fine. I can't breathe, and now these med techs and the hospital staff will see that I'm not fine. Fine is fading fast in the rearview mirror.

I'm full-on panicked. I am totally-losing-it panicked. Like a second-phase spinout strapped to a backboard with my head immobilized, I can't breathe from my chest burning. A new sense of horror as I spin. Will there be an emotional guardrail, or am I going to derail? Jesus. Not a prayer, just a name. Jesus.

Where is Jesus when we spin out of control?

I think his name. Speak his name to my mind. It doesn't work as a sedative. I'm still claustrophobic. I'm still over my stress threshold. Still crying and losing it when we reach the ER. Yes, yes, I would like whatever meds you have to offer. Yes, I am having a panic attack. Yes, the pain and bruising from the seatbelt injury are real. So is the stress, the cost, and the aftermath.

Reflecting days later as I wade through headlines about kidnapped Christians and concerns in my own life, it occurs to me that there is a giant patch of ice lying ahead for Western Christians who have created a theology based on control. Some of you know immediately what I mean.

I've believed it. It's what I heard at church, home, Christian college: follow Jesus. Obey the Bible. Make godly choices. And if you do, the implication is that life will work out, blessings will follow, dreams will come true, and Jesus will always be there for you. That's true, but it isn't the whole truth.

Because there comes a moment when life spins out of control.

In a weak moment, you make a wrong choice. Or maybe it's the loved one who made a wrong choice, who hits the ice patch. But you're in the passenger seat of that loved one's life, spinning out because he or she tried drugs, rejected Jesus, gambled until all was lost, cheated on a spouse, or faced a tragedy not of his or her making.

Maybe you or your loved one made good choices—to serve the Lord on the mission field or the inner city or a small town parish. But tragedy still hits—he or she was raped, kidnapped, subjected to lies over a foolish congregational conflict, fired because he or she wouldn't play a game of the world.

I think about Kayla Mueller's letter home.[2] Kayla was the American humanitarian worker kidnapped, tortured, and killed by ISIS. In her letter, she tells her family her biggest regret is they are suffering, too, because she had found God was there with her. In the suffering, in the spin, there was God.

The whole truth is that Jesus is there in the midst of the spin—when life is out of control and even when we're out of control. The moment I started to lose the panic was when I turned into the spin. I stopped trying to control the moment and my response. I let myself freak out. It's the same advice we give drivers in the snow here in New England—don't fight the spin. Turn into it.

It's right and good to love Jesus, follow him, obey him, trust his word, and make godly choices. But if you base your entire theology on those things bringing about a right and safe result, if your theology is one of control, you're headed for a full-on spinout when the icy patch of persecution arrives on our shores.

The Christians kidnapped by ISIS have lost all earthly control over their lives. They can, perhaps, manage their responses, but if they are tortured, maybe not even that. Still I believe, they'll find Jesus is present in the spin.

Paul writes in 2 Timothy 2:13, "If we are faithless, he remains faithful—for he cannot deny himself" (ESV). I was not full of faith following my accident; I was full of panic. But Jesus remained present with me. He was more real than the guardrail. In the midst of the fear, I knew he would be my spiritual guardrail no matter how I reacted to the spin.

We have every reason to trust Jesus. In the days to come, when the world goes into a full-on spin, our theology will expand and we will see—even when we lose control—Jesus is there.

Small Steps Toward Slaying Giants

1. This chapter is a reminder that we aren't seeking to grow in these qualities in order to guarantee ourselves perfect lives. Trouble will come. While we work at increasing self-control, let's remind ourselves there's much in this world we can't control. Circumstances, however, never throw Jesus. They never catch him off guard. Thank him for his presence through everything.
2. What does Isaiah 43:1-2 say we can endure with Jesus? Have you experienced life going out of control, but God was there? How can you use that experience to encourage others?

❧ ❧ ❧

One Stone for Your Sling: When *fine* is fading fast in the rearview mirror, Jesus is there, even in the spin.

Self-Control

Day Four

One Fear to Rule Them All

Self-Control in Trying Times

I'm not prone to anger, but I felt my ire rise in the days following the *Charlie Hebdo* shooting in Paris.

On January 7, 2015, two men forced their way into the offices of the satirical weekly paper and murdered eleven people, injuring eleven more. People worldwide protested the killings using the slogan *Je suis Charlie,* meaning "I am Charlie."[3]

The outcry was understandable, but what I found aggravating was countless individuals spouting the courageous phrase from their living rooms or from behind safe news desks far from the mayhem. Most of us writing that phrase were in serious need of a reality check. The sad truth is that we often don't stand up for what we believe. We don't stomach telling the truth to our neighbors, never mind to gunmen. We are so not Charlie. I don't agree with all the opinions expressed by the political cartoonists who died, but I do admire their courage in promoting their beliefs publicly despite the threats to their lives. Most people would not have the courage to do what the cartoonists of *Charlie Hebdo* routinely did.

It's a sad state of affairs, these times in which we live. Gas prices are dropping, but the cost of courage is on the rise. Many of us don't have what it takes to be as brave as these days require. I know I don't. I was born scared. The list of things that frighten me grows by the moment and includes stuff that would make you snort with laughter. I strive to apply self-control in handling my multiple fears. Fortunately, one fear rules the rest. Because of that, I sometimes appear courageous to others when, the truth is, I simply have my fears properly prioritized.

That's not true for everyone.

I once spent hours embroiled in a crisis that didn't have to happen. A family's situation reached a boiling point because for months (years, even) well-educated professionals, decent citizens of the family's community, and even Christians chose to stay silent rather than find the courage to say and do hard things to protect a child. There was a lot of tongue clicking, head shaking, self-righteous whispering, and scornful staring, but no one prioritized his or her fears enough to do the right thing.

I didn't want to do it either. Funny how often "the right thing" is painful, complicated, hard, and requires a measure of sacrifice. It took self-control (compliments of the Holy Spirit) to keep silent when the others, who should have acted earlier, thanked me and assured me they'd seen the problem growing for a long, long time. You *what*? You saw this? You sat by waiting for what, exactly?

Revelation 3:15-17 says this, "I know your works. You are neither cold nor hot. I wish that you were either cold or hot. So because you are lukewarm, and neither hot nor cold, I'm about to spit you out of my mouth. After all, you say, 'I'm rich, and I've grown wealthy, and I don't need a thing.' You don't realize that you are miserable, pathetic, poor, blind, and naked." That passage helps me keep my fears in proper order. Such proper order that I appear to have courage.

There's a little girl in Sudan who has her fears in proper order. At thirteen, she was more afraid to take life than to risk her own by refusing to detonate the bomb vest strapped to her by Boko Haram soldiers. They tried to make her a suicide bomber, but she took a stand by refusing to cooperate, risking her own life rather than take others.[4] It boggles the mind, her bravery.

Most of us won't have to face that kind of choice or be called to communicate our convictions on an international stage. That's a relief, since we struggle to state controversial truths to the person across the lunch table at work or across the living room during our small group.

We suppress basic truths that we should speak, such as, "I'd rather you didn't share gossip with me," "Your lifestyle is affecting your child. Either change it or I'll speak to the authorities," or "No, I don't believe there are many paths to God. I believe there is only one, and his name is Jesus."

Ever stumble over words like these? *Vous n'êtes pas* Charlie.

Christians should lead the planet in courage. Why? Because we should have properly prioritized fears. Which of my fears rules the others so I pass as brave? It is my fear of the Lord, my holy reverence for Jesus Christ. I may fear saying hard things, the disapproval of others, causing discomfort, or social leprosy; but more than that, I fear letting down the One who laid down his life for me. This is a healthy fear foremost in the hearts and minds of brave Christians.

Jesus said in Luke 12:4-5, "I tell you, my friends, don't be terrified by those who can kill the body but after that can do nothing more. I'll show you whom you should fear: fear the one who, after you have been killed, has the authority to throw you into hell. Indeed, I tell you, that's the one you should fear."

What about you? Are your fears properly prioritized? If so, you will find courage in the moment you require it. If not, *vous n'êtes pas* Charlie. Learn to exercise self-control over your fear of social disapproval and move onto clinging to the fear of the Lord.

Small Steps Toward Slaying Giants

1. List the things that frighten you—all of them, from spiders to social disapproval to World War III. Is there a fear you believe God can't handle or doesn't already know is coming? Next, write down 1 John 4:4 and repeat it after reading each one of your fears.
2. Read Luke 12. God says many things in this chapter related to managing our fear, anxiety, and speculation about the future. What are some things you can apply this week from this chapter in the way of exerting self-control over your fears?

One Stone for Your Sling: One of my fears rules the rest. Because of that, I sometimes appear courageous to others when, the truth is, I simply have my fears properly prioritized.

Self-Control

Day Five

How Not to Cough Up a Human Hairball

Self-Control for Inner Peace

Recently I learned about a rare disorder called trichophagia. Well, "learned about" might be stretching it.

I was watching a BBC drama series about a doctor in a small village, and one of the characters presented with symptoms that turned out to be trichophagia. The doctor made his diagnosis after his patient dramatically coughed up a hairball.

That's right. Trichophagia is what we call it when someone chews on and eats their own hair. Hair doesn't digest, so it forms hairballs that humans, unlike cats, don't normally cough up on their own. Usually they require surgery. God didn't design the human body to digest hair.

This got me thinking. Well, not about hair, but about anger. He didn't design the human soul to digest anger either.

We like to pretend we have few choices about anger. It's a feeling. It "flares up." It's "uncontrollable." We blame others for our anger: "He made me angry"; "I couldn't help it because she set me off."

God doesn't see anger the way we do. Sure, anger registers on our emotional dashboard, but as soon as it does, God says it's up to us how to respond. Think of anger as a "check engine" light for the soul.

Some of us like to chew on it, ingest it, and try to force it through the belly of a soul that wasn't designed to consume it. Do this often enough and the anger collects and forms a giant hairball in our spirit that we can't cough up. The most skillful of soul surgeons, the Holy Spirit, must remove it before it kills us from the inside out.

Unfortunately, when we're tempted to nurture our anger, we can find plenty of support from others. These days, self-control isn't as highly valued as assertiveness. Forgiveness and long-suffering are poor second cousins to aggressively pursuing what we want and deserve.

It requires significant faith to refrain from anger when its proponents seem justified and so positive it's the only way to reach a desired end. God says differently in James 1:19-20: "Know this, my dear brothers and sisters: everyone should be quick to listen, slow to speak, and slow to grow angry. This is because an angry person doesn't produce God's righteousness."

The writer of Proverbs agreed with James (well, before James existed to be agreed with): "Whoever is slow to anger is better than the mighty, / and he who rules his spirit than he who takes a city" (Proverbs 16:32 ESV) and "Insightful people restrain their anger; / their glory is to ignore an offense" (Proverbs 19:11).

I believe in honesty in relationships, straight talk, and setting limits. Anger, though, is a different animal. God tells us that he is slow to anger, and if our goal is to become like him, then "slow to anger" should be our aim. Anger seems more powerful than patience, long-suffering, forgiveness, or calm assertiveness, but no one is more powerful than God is, and it's not his go-to emotion!

As I work to manage my own emotional storehouse, I know from now on I'll picture this poor guy clutching his stomach in agony and then violently (and disgustingly) coughing up a portion of a hairball just before the rescue unit arrives to take him to the hospital.

God didn't design us to process a steady diet of anger. Best not to chew on it or ingest it in the first place than to let it kill us from the inside out. Wouldn't you agree?

Small Steps Toward Slaying Giants

1. Look up these verses: Numbers 14:18, Psalm 103:8, Nehemiah 9:31, and Exodus 34:6. What is the message of these verses? Does the Lord have sufficient reason to be angry? In all God's wisdom, if anger were the best tool, don't you imagine God would be quick to reach for it? How do these verses fly in the face of the world's impression of God?
2. Read James 1:19-21. How are we to live in regard to anger? Look carefully at this passage and see if you can detect faith, virtue, knowledge, and self-control cooperating with one another again.

One Stone for Your Sling: God did not design the human soul to digest anger.

Self-Control

Day Six

Pray, Reflect, Process, Pray

Ask God to direct you to activities that will give you self-control in increasing measure. Through the ages, Christians have practiced the spiritual discipline of fasting. Many report that engaging in a regular routine of fasting has increased their self-control in other areas. Prayerfully consider incorporating a fast into your week (but consult a physician before beginning any fast). While it's common to fast from food, modern believers find it beneficial to regularly fast from technology or social media.

Reflect on what you've read in his Word this week. Go back to passages that spoke to where you are right now or inspired you to growth. Reread and reflect.

After you've reflected on your chosen Bible passage, engage in a physical or creative activity with the intent of processing what God has said to you through it about self-control. When you finish, ask God to continue the work of building your self-control in increasing measure.

Now, lather, rinse, repeat. In other words, if this works for you, do it with other passages on self-control.

13

Steadfastness in Slippery Times

Steadfastness

Day One

Steadfastness, known by such vexing aliases as *endurance, patience,* or *long-suffering,* is the most underappreciated quality of our faith. We ignore, resist, or dismiss it to our detriment. It can be one of the most powerful beans we bury. The current state of our culture is a testament to people who refused to give up and, eventually, wore everyone else down into accepting their point of view.

Ask anyone who has raised a challenging child. You know the kind I'm talking about—the determined child. The child who keeps asking. The child who won't take no for an answer, repeating his or her requests even under threat of dire consequences. It takes a staunch parent to withstand a steadfast child. Children who won't give up have done in many a determined parent.

Miraculous Perseverance

I've seen steadfastness work in miraculous ways. In my role as a volunteer with seniors, I met a man who complained to me that he struggled with bad mornings and couldn't figure out why. Some days he woke up content with life, but on others he awoke burdened with misery and sadness, struggling to rise. Those days were increasing. I didn't have an answer, but I suggested he confer with me each morning and tell me how he'd spent the prior evening. We would look at the kind of morning it was to see if he could make any connection. All I did was listen and repeat what he told me.

For three weeks, that was how it went. There was nothing fascinating or insightful about our conversations. We met for ten minutes. He described his evening and then how he felt on waking. After the first seven days, he fretted that we didn't have the answer (I certainly had no clue), but I suggested we keep at, if for no other reason than it couldn't hurt.

After two more weeks, he and his wife rushed to see me. He grabbed my hand and shook it repeatedly. "Thank you, thank you, thank you," he gushed. "How can I ever thank you?" His wife stood behind him, nodding and dabbing tears from her eyes. "Do you know what I did last night?"

I had no idea.

"I attended my first Alcoholics Anonymous meeting. Aren't you excited?" he said.

"I may be once I understand the connection. When did you decide you need AA?" I was thoroughly confused.

"It's because of our morning talks. After about ten days, I heard myself saying on the night before my bad mornings that I had some wine. The truth is, on those nights, I had a lot of wine. On the nights before the good mornings, I didn't. At first, I dismissed it, but after two and a half weeks, I couldn't ignore it any longer, and I knew you'd catch on if we kept at it. After three weeks, I asked my wife what she thought about it, and she nearly collapsed with relief that I was seeing what she saw. I'm an alcoholic. It was getting worse, but last night, I turned over a new leaf. Thank you for sticking with me."

He was confident I would have caught on eventually, and maybe I would have, but I hadn't at that point. Fortunately God did, and that made all the difference in his life. Who knows where the situation would have gone if we hadn't persisted and taken a patient, steadfast approach to his problem?

A Crippling Deception

Why do we let Satan convince us steadfastness is boring? Why do we let him deceive us into discounting it? Especially as we see him use it against us! Persistent attacks on us, our families, churches, and communities result in spiritual erosion and moral decay. Evil doesn't mind enduring because it gets the job done. Yet we, God's children, often push endurance aside like the ugly stepchild of Christian virtue.

In Luke 21:10-19, Jesus describes a time of terrible stress, tribulation, and testing. What does he say will save us? Our endurance. Our endurance will gain us our lives. That ought to grab our attention!

Biblically prioritizing endurance can sustain us through hardship because Paul tells us suffering is what produces endurance. Romans 5:3-5 says this, "We even take pride in our problems, because we know that trouble produces endurance, endurance produces character, and character produces hope. This hope doesn't put us to shame, because the love of God has been poured out in our hearts through the Holy Spirit, who has been given to us."

Endurance or steadfastness isn't a glory-seeking virtue, but it serves us well over time and increases our effectiveness and fruitfulness in our knowledge of Jesus.

Word Study Exercise

It's fascinating that John uses the word *steadfastness*, or enduring patience, so often in the Book of Revelation. Read the verses listed here and then summarize why you think God places such a high value on steadfastness in his people: Revelation 1:9; 2:2-3, 9; 3:10; 13:10; 14:12.

Now, work your way back through the other New Testament books and see if your perspective on steadfastness has changed. Write beside each passage what it says about the importance of this virtue:

Romans 15:4-6

2 Corinthians 1:6-7

2 Corinthians 6:3-10

Colossians 1:11

1 Thessalonians 1:3

2 Thessalonians 1:3-4

2 Thessalonians 3:5

1 Timothy 6:11-12

2 Timothy 3:10-13

Hebrews 10:36-39

Hebrews 12:1-3

James 1:2-3

James 5:7-11

Biblical Role Model Ministudy

Many great women of faith have demonstrated patient endurance—certainly Sarah as she waited through decades of barrenness to bear her promised child (Genesis 11–23); Hannah as she petitioned God for her first child (1 Samuel 1); and Abigail, who patiently endured a brutal husband (1 Samuel 25). Men have endured as well: Hosea (Book of Hosea) patiently endured an unfaithful wife; Job (Book of Job) patiently endured relentless loss; and Daniel (Book of Daniel) was steadfast in prayer through decades of captivity. Choose one of these biblical characters and read his or her story. What did this person endure, how did he or she respond to the trials in life, and what was the eventual outcome? See if you can research how long each one waited for deliverance. What does that tell you about God's idea of timing?

Heritage of Faith Walkers

How does patient endurance manifest itself in the lives of historical Christians? How do they respond to God, to challenges, to opposition, to disappointments, to blessings? Joni Eareckson Tada, born in 1949, is a powerful example of endurance. She's an evangelical Christian, author, artist, radio host, and advocate for people living with disabilities. She has sought to serve Christ even as she has endured quadriplegia and breast cancer. Her husband,

Ken Tada, has endured with her. Other examples are the Yazidi women of the Middle East; David Livingstone; Brother Yun; Pastor Saeed Abedini and his wife, Naghmeh Abedini; and Christians living in China, Somalia, or North Korea.

Do you know someone personally who exhibits great endurance? What in this person's life testifies to that trait? What can you learn from him or her about growing in steadfastness?

Small Steps Toward Slaying Giants

1. How do the passages you've read on steadfastness and patient endurance affect your perspective on the trials in your life and the suffering you've experienced? What is the world's perspective on this trait? How can we prevent our minds from being polluted by this perspective?
2. Look at the list of giants in your life. Can you trust God that steadfast endurance in the face of that giant will result in his glory? Armed with perseverance, can you face the giant and watch him shrink even a little? Pray for the strength to endure against the giant.

One Stone for Your Sling: Steadfastness can be one of the most powerful beans we bury.

Steadfastness

Day Two

Thou Shalt Pray Like Sheldon Cooper

Steadfastness in Prayer

I've learned something about prayer from Sheldon Cooper, one of the quirky main characters of *The Big Bang Theory*. It happened when I knocked on heaven's door and realized I sound like Sheldon:

Knock, knock, knock, Jesus?

Knock, knock, knock, Jesus?

Knock, knock, knock, Jesus?

Sheldon is as irritating a character as you'll come across, and yet he's so relentless in his persistence that he moves others to help and support him out of sheer exasperation.

Social relationships baffle Sheldon, and he seeks to manage them by creating contractual agreements with his friends. Hence he has his roommate, Leonard, sign an expansive document referred to as the Roommate Agreement. Even he and his girlfriend have a thirty-one-page relationship agreement. When petitioning his friends for aid, he refers to specific clauses in these agreements, inspiring even reluctant friends to yield.

This concept works both ways as these friends are able to convince Sheldon to step outside his comfort zone (to attend a birthday party or to apologize for wrongdoing) when people explain such action is necessary, as it is a "nonnegotiable social convention."

God brought Sheldon to mind as I meditated over various Bible passages. I marveled that after Cain brought an unacceptable sacrifice to the Lord and then murdered his brother in a fit of jealousy, God granted his request for protection. It appears that God answered his request simply because Cain asked (Genesis 4).

Later that week, I reread the parable of the persistent widow in Luke 18. A cranky judge gives in to a widow's plea for justice simply because she "keeps bothering me": "I will give her justice, so that she will not beat me down by her continual coming." Jesus applies this parable to our prayers saying, "And will not God give justice to his elect, who cry to him day and night?" (vv. 2, 5 ESV).

God brought another passage to mind from Luke 11. Jesus is teaching on prayer and describes a man asleep in bed whose neighbor bangs on his door asking for bread. Jesus says the man doesn't want to rise and doesn't want to help, "yet because of his persistence he will get up and give him as much as he needs" (v. 8 NASB).

Jesus continues his teaching with these words: "And I tell you: Ask and you will receive. Seek and you will find. Knock and the door will be opened to you. Everyone who asks, receives. Whoever seeks, finds. To everyone who knocks, the door is opened" (Luke 11:9-10).

When I was younger, I didn't understand this whole persistence-in-prayer issue, but I'm beginning to have a glimmer now. Some trials, circumstances, and challenges in life arise from deeply embedded spiritual issues—an individual in long-term bondage to sin, a country smothered under spiritual oppression, a heart blinded to Jesus by the idolatry of unbelief. These matters require persistent prayer assault.

Many of us abandon our prayers when God doesn't produce immediate results. How childish and immature are we that we do that? (I'm guilty of this all the time.) God tells us in his Word that there are times when we must petition him in prayer repeatedly. Why? I don't always know, but I believe him when he says it's true. This persistent petitioning demands faith, and the evil one capitalizes on it to mount a counterattack of whispered accusations against the Lord. *He's not coming. He won't answer you. He doesn't care. Give up. You're being foolish. He answers other people's prayers, not yours. You're asking too much. You're not worthy. He's not there.*

All lies, but the effective response to these lies is to pray and not give up.

We should pray like Sheldon. Knock, knock, knock, Jesus? Knock, knock,

knock, Jesus? Knock, knock, knock, Jesus? We, too, can refer to our relationship agreement: "Lord, in Luke 11:9 you said to knock and ask, so I'm knocking and asking."

Don't be surprised if God responds by encouraging us to keep praying using the Sheldon method. When we ask, "Why should we keep praying?" he'll likely answer, "It's a nonnegotiable biblical convention." We should respond like Sheldon Cooper in that moment, too, and reply, "Oh, then by all means, I'll keep praying."

Small Steps Toward Slaying Giants

1. Think about a time you were persistent in prayer. What motivated you, and what was the result? What has caused you to cease praying about something? Is there a problem in your life now but you've abandoned praying for it?
2. Do you know a prayer warrior who is persistent and enduring in prayer? See if this person will talk to you about his or her prayer life and let you in on how he or she prays.

One Stone for Your Sling: Thou shalt pray like Sheldon Cooper.

Steadfastness

Day Three

Strange Testimonies (Stories We Tell in the Desert)

Steadfast While Waiting

When I'm waiting for God to answer my prayers, I like to imagine people from the Bible gathering in an imaginary waiting place swapping stories to pass the time.

Once upon a time, it was testimony night.

The leader poked the fire as the others stared at the flames, the stars, or the shadows on the desert dunes. "Who wants to share? Who's seen God at work this week? Moses? You haven't shared in, you know, ten years."

Moses pulled himself up by his staff and inhaled the damp smoke. "I saw him work in the hills one night a month back. One of my ewes was near death birthing a lamb. I saw the light go clear out of her eyes, so I whispered a prayer to spare her. Next moment, the lamb arrived; and that ewe was licking my hand, as full of life as the day she was born."

Old Caiaphas sighed. "That's it?"

Moses shifted his weight to his other leg. "Well, I still dream about finding a way to help my people, a way to loosen the bondage of their oppression. I talk with the Almighty about it when we're alone out here. But it's been a long time since I ran off."

"You need to let that go, Moses," Caiaphas said. "Maybe that was his plan for you at one point, but you blew it. There's no way you kill a man and then God uses you to help others. You should be grateful for what he's allowed you out here—a quiet life, a little family. Let it go already, brother. That's your testimony. You've been out in the desert twenty years or more. If he was going to use you, he'd have done it by now, wouldn't he?"

Moses sat and Joseph stood. Around one of his ankles was a tether secured to the waistband of another at the fire. Joseph looked at the ground as he spoke. "First, I want to thank Ari the jailer for bringing me out to the fire tonight."

Ari nodded. "You've earned it, Joe. You work hard."

"Thank you. You would think I don't have a testimony from prison, but I have time there to pray and meditate on God's teachings. Some days, although I miss my family, I can't imagine freedom is better than the relationship I share now with the Almighty in the long days of my imprisonment."

Several around the fire grunted. A log popped on the fire.

"There was a time God gave me dreams that said I would be a leader over my brothers. The dreams still come to me. I do believe God has a plan, though that sounds like a prison fantasy now."

Caiaphas nodded. "You sure got a raw deal, kid. We all know about the stunt Potiphar's wife pulled, although I have to say, I can't imagine you weren't leading her on a little. Where there's smoke there's fire, right? God wouldn't have allowed you to be in prison if he didn't think you deserved it somehow.

"Ari says you do well there. Maybe leading prisoners is what those dreams were about. Don't get your hopes up thinking there's more. You're not even a spark in Pharaoh's mind."

As Joseph sat, the leader scanned the group, ignoring one man's upraised hand.

"Ooh, I have a story," the man said, jumping to his feet.

The leader shook his head. "Sit down, Samson. We're talking God-related testimonies, not your newest conquest tale."

"But this one's different! I promise. Her name's Delilah," he said.

The men spoke as one, saying, "Sit down."

Caiaphas looked around. "Hey, where's that runt, Gideon? Are you hiding again, boy?"

The leader lifted a torch and located the young man huddled behind one of the camels. "For Pete's sake, Gideon, there are no Midianites out in this part of the desert. Stand up and testify about seeing God at work."

Gideon shuffled over.

"He said stand up, Gideon," Samson said as he snickered. "Oh, wait, you are standing up!"

Everyone shushed Samson.

"Okay, I do have a testimony, but it's not one you'll believe. He came to me this week. I saw him."

Caiaphas guffawed. "Came to you? Not likely. What did he say?"

"He said, 'The Lord is with you, O mighty man of valor.'"

Samson and Caiaphas rolled with laughter, but the leader silenced them with a glance. "Tell us what else."

Gideon looked off into the desert. "No. I mean, there was more. I asked some questions, but I don't think I can talk about it yet. I'm waiting for confirmation, but until it comes, you'll just think I'm stupid."

"Got that right," said Samson.

Gideon sat, and the group fell into a long silence. The only sound was the scurry of small creatures dashing about and, eventually, Samson's snore.

Moses looked over at their leader and said, "Peter, what made you get this group together, anyway? None of us has any testimony worth telling, but you made it sound important."

Peter smiled as he poked again at the fire. "We're gathered in the desert that lies between vision and fulfillment, between calling and consummation, between visitation and realization, loved ones. It's just as important to pause and tell our stories here as it will be at the end. You don't know that now, but I know it, and there are others who will hang on these words."

"I don't have a vision or a dream or a calling," said Caiaphas. "I'm here out of religious duty. Why did you invite me?"

"Because, old friend, I can't wait to see your face when we tell the ends of our stories. God isn't done with all of us."

The men glanced over at Samson, and Peter's laughter rang out over the dunes. "Even that one, my friends. Wait and see. The best stories have all passed through this desert, trust me."

Is your testimony in the desert between vision and fulfillment? Between calling and consummation? Between visitation and realization, loved one? Gather here, around the fire, and tell what you know. Trust God to bring about the end he desires. One day, we'll tell our stories for a thousand years.

Small Steps Toward Slaying Giants

1. Have you ever felt a dream was dead? Was there a time you despaired that God wasn't even hearing you at all? That all was lost? That you'd never survive your situation? What happened to turn the situation around, or are you still waiting? If you've seen things turn around, how can you use your story to encourage others?
2. What helps you hold on when you're tempted to despair? List Scripture passages that strengthen you, disciplines that uphold you, thoughts that motivate you, and people who support you.

One Stone for Your Sling: We're gathered in the desert that lies between vision and fulfillment, between calling and consummation, between visitation and realization, loved one. It's just as important to pause and tell our stories here as it will be at the end.

Steadfastness

Day Four

One Jesus Story You May Have Missed

Steadfastness in Ministry

Have you ever wondered why Jesus began his work with fishermen?

We get so accustomed to the Jesus story, we don't stop to ask enough questions. What story was Jesus telling us by heading down to the shore to find his first disciples?

He could have started anywhere. He could have chosen from shepherds, rabbis, merchants, musicians, poets, housekeepers, and innkeepers; but he went to the shore in search of his rock, Peter. The Master of communication was surely trying to tell us something with this strategic choice. Something about the task ahead—the task of fishing for men.

I researched what traits make a good fisherman. One article mentioned four: curiosity, consistency, persistence, and good note-taking skills.[1] Look at those characteristics. They speak to someone taking on a task that requires experimentation, endurance, faithfulness, creativity, and a willingness to analyze and learn.

A fisherman faces much hardship in making a living; a person has either to love it or to be committed to it for a higher purpose. Hauling in a loaded net and reeling in a desired catch are brief, fleeting, rewarding moments preceded and followed by hours of back-breaking work, mind-numbing tedium, and crazy-making solitude.

Fishermen are smart in ways the world often discounts. They persist when others return to shore. They brave the cold, the waves, and the labor, but they see the wonders of our Creator that others miss. Frequently misunderstood and underestimated, these men know their efforts often yield little result, so they need faith to wake up the next day and lower their nets again.

Can you hear the story Jesus told when he went to the shore for disciples?

It hasn't gotten any easier—fishing for men. This business to which we're called, this kingdom building, requires calling, passion, and commitment. Perhaps you fish from the pulpit or in a preschool. Perhaps you fish in a foreign land or in the nursery of your own home. You may fish through the creative arts or through the business world, through teaching or through healing. You may haul in nets laden with fish or angle for one catch at a time. It's all hard.

Sometimes you ask yourself, *What if it comes to nothing?*

What if, after all the hard work, sacrifice, self-denial, and risk, the result collapses beneath the weight of your hopes and expectations? That can happen if you're attempting to make that dream appear—to live out his calling on your life. So then you have to ask yourself another question. Right?

What else would I be doing?

How else would I spend my time? If I lay aside the work on this great vision, if I set aside my nets, what pursuits would fill my days? If they appeal to you more—well, go do those things and choose to be someone who finds contentment in accomplishment. Let it be written on your grave: here lies one who achieved every small thing she set out to do.

But if that's not an epitaph you can live with, if you would prefer that your eulogy contains the phrase, "Yes, there was a measure of failure in his pursuits, but every day he aimed at greater things than many dare to dream," then get back to the work. Cast off. Try again.

Bury fear, self-pity, and lesser goals in the shallow grave beneath that first headstone. For you were called to the impossible work even now waiting to be attempted just there beneath your restless hands.

Remember this: even Peter wasn't the Rock until Jesus named him. Jesus chose fishermen so we'd understand the nature of the task—then he transformed them, just as he transforms us.

We have every reason to hope, not in ourselves, but in the One who had a story to tell in his choices down at the shore. What story is he choosing to tell by choosing you?

Small Steps Toward Slaying Giants

1. What failures have you faced in ministry? What long, fruitless stretches have tested your patience, your dedication, or your vision? What got you through those times? What do you do when you feel like quitting? How hard is it to hope when you've worked at something for a long time and seen little or no result?
2. Psalm 107 begins and ends with God's steadfast love, but in between are the stories of people who lost their way until he found them and brought them home. As you read it, ask God to make you more like him, infused with steadfast love for all who have yet to find him.

One Stone for Your Sling: God called you to the impossible work even now waiting to be attempted just there beneath your restless hands.

Steadfastness

Day Five

The Christian You Don't Know

Steadfast in Devotion

She sees me several times a week. I know her views because she makes them known. I am myself with her.

Recently she confessed that she used to hate Christians, but now she's rethinking that: "I think all I knew before were headline Christians, movie Christians, and what my friends say about Christians. You're not like them. I know we disagree, but I don't feel like you hate me. I'm starting to think I might have been wrong about Jesus people."

Thank God. I thought. *Thank you, God, for showing up and showing through all the cracks in my armor.*

It made me wonder what people think we're like on our knees. I wonder if they imagine a prayer life different from the one I have.

When I speak with God in the morning, I'm not asking him to destroy the gay agenda or to wage war against those who made gay marriage legal. When I pray in the morning, I'm asking for strength to meet the challenges of the day, for a filling of the Holy Spirit, and for protection for my loved ones.

With my next prayerful breath, I'm not pleading for him to boost the polls for the political candidate of my choice or to strike another candidate with lightning. I'm pleading for wisdom to do my job and to interact with my loved ones. I'm requesting enough Christlikeness not to hurt or confuse someone before lunch.

As I drive to work, I listen to his Word on CD and then to the headlines on talk radio. When I pray, I'm not calling fire and brimstone down on our enemies or asking God to oppose the heathen masses. I'm requesting the power to obey what I've heard from the Scripture passage and to stay focused despite what I heard from the headlines, which could discourage me to the point of fear or depression. I'm mulling over, with him, what his Word means to me now, today.

By lunch, I thank him for my food but also for patient coworkers. I'm not praying for them to vote the way I vote; I'm praying for healing for a husband's cancer, a job for a son-in-law, reconciliation with an aging mother, and better ears with which to hear their heart needs. I ask for self-control to make healthy choices and healing from the morning's stress.

Through the afternoon, my prayers are sentence brief: Forgive me for losing my cool. Please don't let my car overheat in this traffic. Thank you for the good outcome with that family. Forgive me for that mean thought about that woman. What should I blog about next week? Heal my husband. Watch over my son. Thank you for my daughter. How will we pay that bill?

On the drive home, the issues scream out from the radio news and the callers. Then I pray about what's going on in our culture. I cry out for wisdom. I ask God for patience with us all. I pray for the church to have strength and integrity, for creativity and imagination, for courage and compassion, for the Spirit's power to speak truth and demonstrate love with people who differ from us. No fire. No brimstone. Barely the energy for anger. Lots of pleading. Lots of silent prayers where words fail.

During television viewing and time on social media, I'm asking for strength to resist temptation. Thanking God for joy and laughter. Writing new stories in my head and asking for creative energy. Praying for grandchildren yet to be born that they will know God from the cradle and grow up loving him in a culture at odds with him. Admiring other people's artistic gifts.

When I lay me down to sleep, there are more prayers of confession, more gratitude, and more requests for those I love, family, friends, church, and my town. No holy-war prayers. No culture-war intercessions. No hatred for enemies. I intercede for people near and far who don't follow Jesus yet—individuals and people groups—for God to make himself known to them. I thank God for his mercy and grace.

This is a day in my prayer life, and I know many other believers whose prayers are the same. We love the people in our lives, neighborhoods, country, and world. We love people with whom we differ. We struggle with the great questions facing others. We don't have it together; we need Jesus. Day-by-day. Moment-by-moment.

We are not the worst of us, the loudest of us, the caricatures of us, or portrayals of us by those who misunderstand us. We're sinners saved by grace. Aware of our sinful bent. Grateful for a forgiving God. On fire for him in a way that wants to include others in the joy of him.

What did you think we were?

Small Steps Toward Slaying Giants

1. Psalm 37 is a strong encouragement to remain steadfast and calm and to stay the course even when it appears evil is having its way. Summarize the message of this psalm in your own words. Try writing your own paraphrase verse by verse and ask God to help you live these words today.
2. Do you pray throughout your day? Try it. If necessary, set your phone alarm or watch to remind you, or pray every time you see a particular bird or a stop sign. Use simple, one-sentence prayers, but try to stay in touch with God all day.

One Stone for Your Sling: We are not the worst of us, the loudest of us, the caricatures of us, or portrayals of us by those who misunderstand us. We're sinners saved by grace.

Steadfastness

Day Six

Pray, Reflect, Process, Pray

Ask God to direct you to activities that will give you steadfastness in increasing measure. Choose one of the pressing "giants" in your life and devote yourself to praying for the next forty days for God to work against that giant. Pray every day using your own words or words from Scripture. Don't give up. At the end of forty days, if the giant persists, pray for another forty.

Reflect on what you've read in his Word this week. Go back to passages that spoke to where you are right now or inspired you to growth. Reread and reflect.

Reflect as you move around, engage in an activity, or create something that reflects the passage you've read. Ask God to continue the work of building your patient endurance in increasing measure. Now, lather, rinse, repeat.

14

Godliness for Giant-Killers

Godliness

Day One

When my children were young, my husband traveled a lot for work. Being home alone for days with two children under five is a challenge not for the faint of heart. Early on, I taught them the importance of giving Mommy uninterrupted time with God every morning (not usually first thing, but I generally made it before noon). I told my son that while my children had to listen to me, I had to listen to God. God was really in charge of our household, and he cared deeply that little children are cared for properly. God is the one who made sure Mommy followed his rules and was a good mom. When I spent daily time with Jesus (and a large, hot, black coffee), I listened to what God wanted me to do in the day, just as the two of them listened to me.

I didn't realize how deeply impressed Zack had been with this process until one particularly trying afternoon. Zack was always a determined child with strong ideas about how to spend his days, ideas that rarely included chores, personal hygiene rituals, or naps. If the afternoon was trying, it's likely he was the source. I was losing my mommy cool and had been raising my voice and threatening dire consequences when Zack came into the kitchen with my Bible and my coffee mug.

"Here, Mom," he said, his voice a stage whisper to keep his younger sister from overhearing. "I think you maybe need an extra talk with God. I'll take care of Hannah while you check with him to see if you maybe didn't hear right when he said what to do today."

The understanding that someone was watching over the someone who watched over them helped my children grow up with a sense of security and respect for God's authority. I hope it taught them the importance of dependence on God in all things. (I know they understand the vital need for coffee and time in God's Word.)

Designed for Godliness

God coded into our DNA an understanding that the proper order of things is for humans to be subject to our Creator God (though sinfulness suppresses that truth). This is evident in that even those who don't acknowledge the existence of God are quick to point out hypocrisy in Christians. Even if they don't respect our faith or believe in our God, something in them knows if we do believe in God, we should obey him and live lives reflective of his godliness. Those who say they are in God's family should conduct themselves with godliness. It reflects back on our Father and speaks to our connection with him, our association with him, and to his effect on our character. I grew up in a small town and have recently moved back. My husband was the driver for returning to this tiny village in our tiny state, but he had no idea what it was like to live where everyone knows your name. I learned from childhood that everything I did would get back to my parents and that family reputations were worth their weight in johnnycakes. One of the first things anyone from a small town does is ask questions to establish a person's context and connection to others in the town.

"Stanley? Are you related to Chief Stanley, or are you the sister of Gary from Richmond?"

"Johnsons? Of the Rockville Johnsons or the Hillsdale Road Johnsons? You don't look like a Johnson. Who was your mother?"

"When did you say you moved here? Twenty years ago? Whose house you livin' in? The old Kenney farmhouse? How'd you come by that?"

My husband has had his share of annoyances now that he's had a taste of living where everybody's in your business. "How did people know at the convenience store I was working on so-and-so's roof?" "Someone told your dad I bought a snow-blower and haven't put it in the garage. Wanted him to warn me to get it under cover! That's not your dad's business. Why are they telling him?"

I smile and nod. Yes. You're now living in a place where people take note of your actions and those actions reflect on your entire clan. It is my father's business because this is his town and you are his son-in-law, and that's how it works. You didn't mind it when someone called to mention your daughter was holding hands with a boy down by the bridge, did you?

Reflecting Our Father

The word Peter uses in 2 Peter 1:6 (ESV) that is translated as "godliness" is *eusebeia,* meaning reverence, respect, piety toward God, godliness.[1] Talk about countercultural! An argument could be made that we live as one of the most irreverent generations in modern history. The act of exhibiting reverence or godliness in these times takes courage, conviction, and patient endurance (see the previous chapter for help with this.)

What we often downplay when talking about godliness is that one must be a student of God in order to understand this quality. We often devise a form of godliness that looks nothing like the actual, living God. If we're going to be godly, we must know what godly looks like. The only place to learn that is from the one true God, Jesus Christ.

Word Study Exercise

This is a great opportunity to see how the characteristics work together. Read 1 Timothy 4. Paul references godliness and reverence in this passage, but he also encourages Timothy to draw on faith, virtue, knowledge, endurance, and steadfastness. These aren't isolated characteristics. They're ingredients that combine to create the mature spiritual condition of, not a good Christian, not a perfect Christian, not a magic Christian but an effective, fruitful Christian. List the places in this passage you see each quality referenced.

Now, read 1 Timothy 6. Again, you'll note this passage focuses on godliness and reverence, but see if you can find sections that reference the other qualities we've studied so far. Just as the systems of a living being all work together to support the effective living of that being, so these qualities work together in the believer.

Finally, read 2 Timothy 3. Why is this characteristic such a challenge to live out in these times? Did you notice that verse 5 makes reference to the fact this virtue can be counterfeited? Without faith that would be terrifying, but we are people of faith. This is a strong reminder God has no desire for us to appear godly. His plan, his heart, his powerful transformative effect is for us actually to be godly.

Biblical Role Model Ministudy

Two New Testament figures loom large as godly men: Peter and Paul. Choose one to research.

Peter plays a significant role in the Gospels and Acts 1–15, and he authored 1 and 2 Peter.

Paul first appears on the scene in Acts 7:58 under his original moniker, Saul. He joined the family and was reborn as Paul in Acts 9. His story continues through the Book of Acts, and he authored at least thirteen books of the New Testament.

If you're short on time, read just a couple of key stories about them. Peter got out of the boat and walked on water with Jesus in Matthew 14. Matthew 26 records his denial of Jesus, and John 21, his restoration. In Acts 4, Peter and John stand before the council in Jerusalem.

Saul witnesses the stoning of Stephen in Acts 7 and persecutes the early church in Acts 8. In Acts 9, Saul meets Jesus on the Damascus road and becomes a believer, referred to from Acts 13 forward as Paul. If you still believe developing these characteristics will protect you from trials, read Acts 27 and see what Paul endured on his voyage to Rome.

Whichever apostle you choose, make note of every story that reveals one of the character traits to which Peter refers in 2 Peter 1:1-10. Relish any of the stories that reveal neither of these men was perfect. This isn't a pursuit of perfection but a pursuit of the person of Christ that results in effective, fruitful living.

Heritage of Faith Walkers

C. S. Lewis (1898–1963)—British novelist, academic, theologian, and Christian apologist who authored numerous classics of the Christian faith—is an example of godliness known to many Christians. He served in WWI, lived through WWII, and survived the death of his wife, Joy Davidman, from bone cancer in 1960. Others who exemplified godliness are Oswald Chambers, Martin Luther, Fanny Crosby, Eric Liddell, and Hilda of Whitby. Ask others from your faith community for their favorite faith walkers and start a list. Be inspired by their lives and practices. Who is a good example of godliness in your own faith community? Invite him or her to share a testimony to encourage your own growth in this characteristic.

Small Steps Toward Slaying Giants

1. What does God tell us about himself in Exodus 34:1-7 and Job 38–42? What then is it like to be like him?
2. All great giant-slayers from Caleb and Joshua to David could have seen the giants before them from their own perspective but chose to see the giants from a godly perspective. Think of the giants in your world and all you've studied so far. What do they look like from your perspective, and what do they look like from God's?

One Stone for Your Sling: What we often downplay when talking about godliness is that one must be a student of God in order to understand this quality.

Godliness

Day Two

What Do You Get When You Interrupt Jesus?

Godliness of Agenda

Interruptions used to make me crazy.

I like to feel, every day, that I've accomplished something. Interruptions interfere with that sense of accomplishment.

Modern life-management advice revolves around goal setting: Know what you want to achieve. Set goals. Create objectives. Avoid distractions. Minimize interruptions. Accomplish goals. Enjoy success.

Sounds like a beautiful plan.

In fact, some people advise determining five-year plans. This is popular advice not only for individuals but also for churches and ministries. For the most part, I agree that setting goals is worthwhile. Yet I'm impressed with how many of the stories the gospel writers tell about Jesus emerged from interruptions. I can't imagine anyone accusing Jesus of not being goal oriented, but his days don't read like someone trying to accomplish something. Most of the great stories we know of his life result from interruptions.

Jesus was enjoying a wedding in Capernaum when his mom interrupted him with their wine-shortage problem. His first miracle was in response to an interruption. A Pharisee named Nicodemus sought Jesus out after dark, interrupting whatever other plans Jesus had, to learn he must be born again. On the way to Galilee, Jesus paused at a well and asked a Samaritan woman for a drink. She asked him questions, and an interruption became an open door for the Samaritans to the gospel. On his way to heal Jairus's daughter, a woman who had been bleeding for twelve years interrupted Jesus. He not only healed her but also took the time to stop and speak with her. A sinful woman interrupted a Pharisee-hosted meal to wash Jesus's feet with her tears, anoint them with perfume, and display her adoration. Jesus announced her story would be remembered always. You have to believe Jesus's original agenda, for every day was never anything banal or useless to begin with; but still, he never blinked at an interruption.

We know Jesus made a habit of rising early to pray, and we know he traveled the countryside preaching and healing. We know he was in great demand, but he greeted interruptions as opportunities, trusting them as divine appointments. Looking at even more biblical stories through this lens, we see that, alternately, God is constantly interrupting someone's life with his own plans.

He interrupted Moses with a burning bush. He interrupted Joseph with time in a pit and a prison. He interrupted Esther when King Ahasuerus appropriated her for his harem. He interrupted Mary and Joseph amid their plans to marry and enjoy a simple life. He interrupted Paul on the way to Damascus. While none of them had five-year plans for their ministries or even their lives, many of them did make paying attention to God their daily goal.

Here's the takeaway for me: my chief goal in life is to make myself available to God every day—that is, to show up before him in prayer, in study of his Word, in obedience, and in listening to his Holy Spirit. Therefore I can trust that what I see as interruptions are divine appointments.

I believe I should work toward the greater goals I've prayerfully developed but with an awareness that God is in the *now*. He *is* in this moment, and if I want to be with him, I must be *here*, not pressing on to the next moment while he lingers with a soul in need of Christ. It seems awfully backward to tap my toe impatiently while Jesus chats with someone who is interrupting "progress" toward my goals.

I imagine Jesus drove the disciples a little crazy with his constant attention to interruptions. I'm right there with them. Drives me nuts, too. That's because I want my life to look like something. Making my life "look like something" doesn't even show up on Jesus' to-do list.

What would happen if tomorrow you asked God to open your eyes to the opportunities in the interruptions? I've been doing that more and more—that is, releasing my need to feel accomplished and making myself available to God in the moment.

J. R. R. Tolkien wrote, "Not all those who wander are lost."[2] I have to believe not all those who are interrupted are off task.

Explore the freedom of the ministry of interruptions. Dare to be like Jesus and put your day into the hands of the Master. What do you get when you interrupt Jesus? You get a divine appointment; a glimpse of God; the hands, feet, and heart of the gospel; and the kingdom of God here and now.

Small Steps Toward Slaying Giants

1. Try it. Embrace the interruptions. Not sold yet? Read one of the Gospels and count the number of stories based on interruptions to Jesus's day.
2. Remember a time when something that came into your life unexpectedly and without your plan turned out to be an adventure or a gift from God. Share that story with someone else to encourage him or her.

One Stone for Your Sling: Not all who are interrupted are off task.

Godliness

Day Three

Why Women Should Not Rule the World

Godliness of Perspective

The gentleman across from me is highly evolved, or so he explains to me.

He tries to make that apparent by sporting a ponytail and wearing a sweater vest. When I speak, he is intensely interested in what I have to say. He emphasizes this with laser-pointer eye contact and frequent, thoughtful nods. I'm brilliant when I'm speaking with this man.

Then he opens his mouth. "I imagine you're not accustomed to men of my generation really listening to you and appreciating your opinion as a woman."

I try to protest, but he's not listening.

"I have such deep admiration for women that most of my closest friends are women. I truly believe all of humanity would be better served if we handed over the reins of leadership in all areas of life to women."

He pauses here so I can express my undying gratitude for his validation of my gender. That's not what I do. "Tell me more about why you believe women should become the leaders of the world to the exclusion of all men."

He's taken aback at my question. As if I'm asking him to explain why children prefer candy to broccoli or why the ground is wet after a good rain. "Why, women, by nature, are smarter, wiser, and gentler than men. They are nurturers, life givers, and lovers. Men are cutthroat, impulsive, mean-spirited, war mongering, and territorial. Women have no such inclinations!"

"Ha!" I exclaimed to his shock. "You, sir, have never been inside a junior high girls' locker room!"

Our conversation ended right after that. Ponytail-sweater-vest man walked away deflated, but nothing I'm sure that couldn't be corrected by a cup of herbal tea and a chat with his circle of wise, earth-mother, world-dominating women friends. He will tell them about me, and soon they'll all be sending positive corrective thoughts my way and having themselves a quiet chuckle because I'm not as evolved as they are.

Seriously.

I'm going on record here to say I like men. Some of my best friends are men. I also like women and have a wide circle of female friends. It's popular to espouse the virtues of women over men, but really, I have inhabited the planet for more than fifty years now and have seen troublemakers wearing dresses and troublemakers wearing pants. Some of them were even men.

I saw a teacher leading a group of first-graders on a field trip. This instructor proudly sported a button on her coat that stated "Girls Rule, Boys Drool." I had to stop her and ask if she didn't feel that sent the wrong message to the little boys in her charge.

"First off," she began, with no small amount of arrogance, "most of the boys in the group can't read yet [as if it was their fault], and second off, it's an important message for them to get early on in life. They've been dominating and oppressing for way too long."

I glanced sadly at the tiny world dominators she was trying to keep in place. Maybe there was a Stalin among them, but if so, he was about twenty years away from a good mustache, never mind being an oppressor of the confident Amazonian girls in his class.

Here's my point. This woman-as-demigod thing has gotten out of hand. It may be up to us women to call it to a screeching halt. I can read history—I've lived a great deal of it myself—and there's no place for men to look down on, abuse, oppress, or denigrate women. Period. Because that's right and fair, not because women are better than they are! It's not putting my gender down to state that women are no better than men are; it's simply stating a biblical truth. God is evenhanded in Scripture when he labels us all sinners.

Eve took the first bite of fruit, but unless I missed that part in which she wrestled Adam to the ground and force-fed him, he was munching right along with her within moments. We all inherited the same sinful nature, an equal capacity for evil, an equal condemnation apart from Jesus Christ, an equal penchant for distortion and dysfunction of what we were designed to be. Brace yourself. This means that women have the capacity for evil and they know how to use it.

I've heard countless women quote this verse from Paul's letter to the Galatians: "There is neither Jew nor Greek; there is neither slave nor free; nor is there male and female, for you are all one in Christ Jesus" (Galatians 3:28). But I've never heard one of them use it to defend a man.

I'm grateful that God designed me as a female. I've had more than my share of run-ins with the opposite sex. Still, when I look in the mirror, I see a sinner saved by grace—one who wears mascara, but a sinner still. I am fortunate enough to be invited to join the family of God, a family that includes brothers I've grown to love. I don't think women should rule the world. I think God should do it by using women and men who know him and understand his ways.

Small Steps Toward Slaying Giants

1. Read Romans 12:1-3. What is the risk addressed by these verses, and what is the reward for obedience? What is the process by which our minds are transformed? Read James 1:19-27. What are ways we prevent being polluted by the world? Is there a step you need to take this week to encourage yourself is this area?
2. Read Galatians 2:11-21. Here Paul writes about a time when he confronted Peter on the way he behaved based on some worldly thinking. When has someone confronted you, and how did you handle it? When have you exhorted someone else and there was a positive outcome? What help can we be to one another in this process of transformation?

One Stone for Your Sling: I don't think women should rule the world. I think God should do it by using women and men who know him and understand his ways.

Godliness

Day Four

I Wrote This Chapter Standing on My Desk

Everyday Godliness

I know you can't see me right now, but as I write this, I'm standing on top of my desk.

From here, I'm reenacting the scene from *Dead Poets Society* in which English teacher John Keating encourages his students to stand atop their desks in order to gain a fresh perspective. That is what I need every day to live grace and light in a shadowy world. When my view remains tethered to the earth, my soul senses the strain as it yearns for the heights God designed it to know.

With the sword supplied by my armor in Christ, I sever the sandbags of limited perspective and see life from atop the desk in God's classroom. Written there on the board in stardust chalk is the phrase *Coram Deo*—translated as "in the presence of God,"[3]—for that is the lesson of the day for this day and each day I care to pay attention.

To live *Coram Deo* is to live one's entire life in the presence of God, under the authority of God, to the glory of God. Alice stepped through her looking glass, and Lucy had her wardrobe; but I have before me the open door of heaven entered through the cross of Christ. Their doors are contained in stories, but my door is the entrance to the original Story, the true Story, the only never-ending Story, and the Author weaves in a plotline just for me.

In entering into relationship with Jesus, I entered this Story. While my feet continue to touch the gritty pavement of this world, my soul abides in the reality of that classroom. Every day that I live with an awareness of his presence is a day I appropriate my eternal life now.

What choices can I make with my time now that I will celebrate having made on the day I fully enter eternity? What are the ways I can spend my time that I will never regret?

I won't regret a single breath spent on prayer. Not one.

Once I prayed for a girl trapped in a vicious cycle of spiritual bondage. The girl walked away from the prayer apparently unchanged. One year later, she testified that from the moment of that prayer, she was free to change. It took her time to inhabit that change, but she realized her freedom in that moment in prayer. I just hadn't seen it.

How many other prayers that seem, from behind this earthly veil, to be impotent are actually at work in others' lives? It helps me to imagine my prayers rooted in the fertile soil of eternity. When I arrive home with Jesus, I will see this prayer tree with the roots of thanksgiving and the lush, leafy arms of praise, the sap of confession flowing freely through its trunk, and hanging like ripe pomegranates from each branch, the fruit of my intercessions.

I won't regret a single moment I told the truth. Not one.

Not even when that truth was ignored or rejected. Not even when it was greeted by mocking or derision. Not even if it resulted in my harm. From space, satellites capture the lights that human populations emit on earth. From the heavens, the great cloud of witnesses track the light produced each time one of us testifies to truth. When a believer is scraped against this flinty world, the spark of truth produced can set a blaze that is a testimony for Christ to all the heavenly host.

Finally, I won't regret even the feeblest attempts I've made to love as God loves me. Not even one.

I'm bad at it. It's a clumsy thing, my loving others. The victims of my attempts at love don't always appreciate the effort, but even the raw scribbles of the child da Vinci, were they discovered today, would be treasured because we would see them as the early works of a master. When I see God face to face, I'll notice that my first attempts to love as he loved are taped to his refrigerator.

Today I invite you to rise up from your place on this earth and join me on the desk in God's classroom. Can you, too, see eternity from here? What choices you make now will you be glad you made on the day you see him face to face?

Small Steps Toward Slaying Giants

1. Read 1 Corinthians 2 and consider why people who don't know Christ don't share your perspective on the issues of the day. How does this inform your prayers for them? How can this work to keep you from being discouraged?
2. List three ways you can invest your time that you won't regret. What Scripture passage assures you that God approves of this activity? How can this help you determine your schedule for your days this week and say no to other things?

❧ ❧ ❧

One Stone for Your Sling: When a believer is scraped against this flinty world, the spark of truth produced can set a blaze that is a testimony for Christ to all the heavenly host.

Godliness

Day Five

Christianity Will Not Save You

Godliness of Religion

God told Hosea to marry a prostitute, so right out of the gate you know you're not dealing with an ordinary God.

Jehovah is no God we'd create. We don't have it in us to fashion One so complex and yet nuanced; so dramatic, yet subtle; so just, yet merciful; so holy, yet loving; so endlessly creative, beautiful, inventive, and strong.

The gods humanity makes are one dimensional, ham-handed, and either distant or faulty. They're crudely drawn and given bumbling monikers like Sun God, God of Thunder, Zeus, Gaia, or modern versions named after dead men. We scaffold them so they won't fall, with religious systems of rituals and rules that followers carefully observe to avoid disfavor.

They demand tributes. They accept bribes. They are mute or dead or conjured through spells. The individual lives of humans are meaningless to the gods of our creation. They bless peoples, nations, and sects. They like large numbers, mobs, and armies. They are impressed by grand gestures like suicide bombs and slain enemies.

God—the true God—knows your name.

He knew Hosea. He knew the whore the prophet married, Gomer. He named their children. He knew the story that he planned their lives to tell, and it was like no other. The thread of their plotline was different from Gideon's, which varied from Rebekah and Isaac's, which was unlike Hannah's.

But we persevere in foolishness, we Jesus followers. Sometimes we covet other gods who are no gods. We like the checklists in their systems. We envy the promise of their rituals. We fear the numbers in their armies. Therefore we create a phantom faith that has the appearance of following Jesus, but really, it's a system known by a name like any other false god, *the Christian religion.*

It looks like holiness, appropriates Jesus's name, and brilliantly counterfeits the reality of God, but it cannot save us. It's become a cliché, but it's a worthwhile truth: those who follow Jesus do not participate in a religion; we engage in a relationship with the living God. If you're practicing a religion, return to God's Word and seek Jesus.

God—the true God—gave us the rules of holiness to school us in our unrighteousness. That was their purpose. He knew they wouldn't save us, but he knew we wouldn't seek salvation if we thought we were fine. So he created a perfect mirror called the Law. His intent was not to spiral us into endless self-reflection but to make us hungry for a beauty and perfection we can attain only in Jesus.

For too long, I fell prey to the phantom faith. I succumbed to an evangelical angst that left me skittish, like a soldier hiking miles through unmapped minefields. As soon as I nailed the big rules, someone showed me the finer points on which I failed. Then when I made progress on those, I came to see my inner being could devise sins not specifically listed. I was always blowing up.

This became an endless cycle of pursuit and despair until Jesus pried my fingers loose from the phantom faith, the false following, the Christianity that isn't about Christ, and he set me free. All the religions we create are prisons, pathways leading in endless labyrinths until we drown in our own reflections. They do not lead to glory.

If Hosea and Gomer showed up at some churches today, telling the story of how Gomer chases after other men but Hosea always pursues her and wins her back because God has a story to tell with their lives, they'd be handed a brochure for a marriage workshop weekend and told to sit quietly until they work out their issues.

I'm not saying I'd be the first to grab Hosea's hand and show him to the pulpit to preach, but I like to think I'd listen to his story, pray for discernment, and open God's Word with him to seek direction on how best to make his message known.

We like our gods to fit into neat boxes, but God's message as told in his Word isn't a tidy thing. It has an order, yes, but there is a wildness to it, like the woolly prophets crying out in the wilderness, shunned by Pharisees, screaming into the wind.

God's story is so vast, so great; he winds a plotline into each of our single lives and weaves us like thread into his great story—those who follow Jesus, that is. He's not like any God we'd create. He's not enthralled with numbers. He commands us to love our enemies. He poured his system, his law, his prophets, his Word into his Son, Jesus, and said we should follow him.

Yes, we do this from inside communities called churches. Yes, we call ourselves Christians. Yes, he calls us to obey his Word as revealed in Scripture. But we must beware the phantom faith of thinking we save ourselves through attendance, checklists, or prescribed pathways. There is only One Way, Jesus.

A time is coming when the counterfeit will look remarkably like the real. We must train ourselves in truth now, by studying God's Word and by knowing his Son. Feasting on his Word now while it may be found will train our souls' palate to distinguish between Christ and the phantom faith.

Our God is not like any we would create. He tells his story through prophets and whores. He rides on the clouds and cooks fish on the seashore. He weeps. He dies for sinners. He rises from death and lives forevermore.

Reject all created gods. There is One who revealed himself to those he Created, more magnificent than our imaginations could devise. Serve him alone, and taste life, truth, freedom, and light.

Small Steps Toward Slaying Giants

1. Read Hosea 1–3. How does God approach his unfaithful bride, Israel, in order to reclaim her? What does that tell us about God's love and mercy? Hosea 2:14-23 describes how God will act. It mentions his steadfast love. Think back to our chapters on steadfastness or patient endurance. Take time to tell God what it means to you that his love is steadfast and that he extends to us his patient endurance.
2. Colossians 2:20-23 and James 1:25-27 describe God's perspective on religion. Why is the distinction between following a religion and being in relationship with Jesus so vital? How can we keep ourselves aligned with Jesus and not fall into a religious trap?

❧ ❧ ❧

One Stone for Your Sling: All the religions we create are prisons, pathways leading in endless labyrinths until we drown in our own reflections. They do not lead to glory.

Godliness

Day Six

Pray, Reflect, Process, Pray

Ask God to direct you to activities that will give you godliness in increasing measure. One way to increase godliness is to spend hours with God. If you can, devote an entire day to getting alone with him in nature, reading his Word, singing praise, and enjoying him. If there's no way to make space for that right now, try turning off your radio, television, and other media for a day. Make use of the quiet spaces this creates in the margins of your daily routine to read a Bible verse, hum a hymn, or sit and pray in a sunny place.

Reflect on what you've read in his Word this week. Go back to passages that spoke to where you are right now or inspired you to growth. Reread and reflect.

After you've reflected on your chosen Bible passage, engage in your preferred activity with the intent of processing what God has said to you through it about godliness. Ask God to continue the work of building your godliness in increasing measure. Lather, rinse, repeat. If this works for you, do it with other passages on godliness or sections of the book that spoke to you.

15

Brotherly Affection with Backbone

Brotherly Affection

Day One

My kid brother was a rascal. Like Calvin from *Calvin and Hobbes,* he was funny, smart, and always up to something. He also seemed to have nine lives because he pulled some crazy stunts but came out alive, smelling like popularity. I was serious, studious, and afraid of my own shadow. What a pair!

Waiting for the bus one day, my brother decided to play with a bumblebee. He impressed the other kids with his fearlessness at capturing the bee barehanded and waving it at all of us.

"Put it down," I scolded, as only big sisters can. "You're going to get stung."

"Ooh, does that scare you?" he taunted. "Look, ooh, Lori, a wittle bee's going to sting me! Oh, no!"

I stuck my nose back into my book and ignored him. When the bus arrived, I hurried on with my brother after me. It was a full morning on the bus, so he was stuck sitting beside me. Suddenly I felt a raging heat in my thigh, as though someone had stuck me with a syringe full of chili sauce. "Ow, ow, ow, what's going on?" I cried out to everyone's entertainment. I raised my skirt high enough to see an angry red welt forming around—what else?—a bee sting!

I glared at my brother. "How did this happen? Where is that bee?"

Red-faced and chagrined, he pointed at his jacket pocket. "I killed it before we got on the bus. Honest, it was dead. Then I stuck it in my pocket. How did I know it could sting even after it was dead?"

That story captures both our relationship and our personalities. He would do risky things and come out fine. I would play life safe and end up stung by a dead bee hidden in his pocket.

So you'll excuse me if, when I hear the term *brotherly affection* (2 Peter 1:7 ESV), I don't get all misty-eyed and cuddly. Brotherly affection around these parts was a less delicate thing—more roughhousing, teasing, and trouble than quiet board games, shared confidences, and warm hugs. Still, we're available for each other. Even as adults, we have very different perspectives, but there's a bond between us that will remain forever. We share memories no one else does (even when we remember them differently). We witnessed each other's childhood. We defend each other against outsiders even if we agree with them. We celebrate each other's joys, but we also tell each other hard truths.

It's About Commitment

I actually think this is what God is going for when he commands us to be ever increasing in brotherly affection. He isn't trying to get us to be nice to one another at church. We've perfected that art—sometimes to our detriment. Instead, he's trying to incite us to commit to one another. He wants us to understand there's no escaping family. He's sending the message that we don't have a say in whom he includes in our family, but he expects us to learn to love one another anyway. He wants us to get real, to know one another so well we can call each other out on our *stuff*.

Siblings have long-term relationships that wax and wane. We didn't choose each other, but we know each other in ways no one else does—even when we aren't close. My brother and I aren't buddies, but there's a way he knows me and I know him that no one else does. There are siblings who are best friends. And there are siblings who won't give one another the time of day, but that doesn't sever the ties that bind them. That's how it is in the church.

Brotherly affection isn't limited to our relationships within the church, but it does start there. To grow in brotherly affection, then, is to increase our commitment to our brothers and sisters in Christ despite knowing them well, seeing their faults, differing with them, and even suffering hurts inflicted by them. When we're children, we don't appreciate siblings. That's something we need maturity to recognize.

Learning to Love

My son was an only child until he was four. Shortly after his sister was born, she was napping in her infant carrier as Zack snuggled onto the sofa between his father and me. "This is great, isn't it?" he said. We agreed. "Don't you think it would be even better if *she* wasn't here?"

Well, of course, we didn't, but we understood siblings can be an acquired taste and knew that, as years passed, he would learn to appreciate having Hannah around.

We worship a perfect God, but as a church, we fail one another sometimes. Just as I was stung by my brother's dead bee, so we wound one another. We disappoint and frustrate one another. Occasionally we search for a spiritual DNA test to determine if someone claiming to be a sibling truly is. God reminds us that sorting us out is his business, not ours (Matthew 13:24-30). His call to love covers everyone from friend to foe, leaving no wiggle room on treating even the irritating members of the family of God with compassion and respect.

Brotherly affection requires constant work, commitment, and growth. Just as my son didn't appreciate his sister when he was a toddler but grew to as he matured, so our lack of appreciation for brothers and sisters in Christ betrays a lack of spiritual maturity. This isn't to say we always agree with or enjoy uninterrupted fellowship with all believers. That isn't real. Part of being in a family is working out differences, forgiving hurts and failures, and understanding there are times we must all go to our separate rooms and think about what we've done.

Loving Beyond Family

Working from the family model also helps our perspective on relating to those who aren't in relationship with Jesus. As we grow in brotherly affection, it spills over to include all those in the human family. Healthy families seek friendships outside their immediate relatives and expect not to spend every waking moment together. But they do prefer one another at important times and make a habit of gathering regularly unless separated by distance for important callings.

Of course it's healthy for Christians to build relationships with those not in the family of God, but God warns us to care especially for one another's needs (Galatians 6:10). God doesn't expect us to be exclusively involved with his family, but we're to be committed to one another in a special way.

Showing brotherly affection to those outside the family of God includes serving them in ministry, respecting them as people made in God's image, and speaking the truth to them at all times, even when they don't want to hear it. Brotherly affection isn't about flowery cards and eloquent wedding toasts. It's a blessed tie that binds us no matter how much we strain against the connection, disagree, or choose favorites. Exhibiting brotherly affection is not optional for the believer, so commit to growing in this area. Don't make Jesus pull this church over!

Word Study Exercise

In 2 Peter 1:7, Peter uses the Greek word *philadelphia,* meaning fraternal affection, brotherly love.[1]

List the ways God commands us to actively love one another in the following passages.

Romans 12:3-21
1 Peter 1:13-25
Hebrews 13:1-17

Apparently, the church in Thessalonica is one to study because, according to Paul in 1 Thessalonians 4:1-12, they had no need for anyone to teach them about brotherly affection because they were so practiced in it. It's worthwhile then to read 1 and 2 Thessalonians in one sitting to get a feel for them and their practices. List their behaviors and consider how you can integrate more of them into your relationships.

Biblical Role Model Ministudy

Choose to research one of these biblical figures who exhibited fervent brotherly affection: Jonathan loved David like a brother; follow the story of their friendship in 1 Samuel 18–31. The sweet, short story of Dorcas is in Acts 9:36-42. John refers to himself as "the disciple whom he loved." It's interesting to read references to him in Jesus's final days on earth and see what actions resulted from their brotherly affection as Jesus endured the cross (John 19:26, 20:2, 21:7, 21:20).

Heritage of Faith Walkers

One Christian to study in order to learn about brotherly affection is Dr. Helen Roseveare, the English medical missionary who served in the Congo. She returned there to minister after recovering from five months of imprisonment by rebel forces in 1964, which included severe maltreatment. Others known for this quality are Francis of Assisi, Philip Yancey, Max Lucado, Mother Teresa, and Brenda Salter McNeil. Encourage those in your faith community who excel in brotherly affection.

Small Steps Toward Slaying Giants

1. In what ways have others within the church shown brotherly affection to you that were particularly meaningful? How have you seen Christians act toward people outside the church that demonstrated brotherly affection? How do you best show your brotherly affection toward others? In what areas can you grow in this trait?
2. Sometimes the "giants" we have to topple reside within us. Racism, bitterness, unforgiveness, and resentment can lead to hardening of the heart and isolation from brothers and sisters in Christ. They can cripple our ability to love others outside the family of God, too. How could growing in brotherly affection help you topple these particular giants or make your heart an inhospitable place for them to survive?

One Stone for Your Sling: God is trying to incite us to commit to one another.

Brotherly Affection

Day Two

The Day I Realize I Don't Love You

Everyday Brotherly Affection

Dear unbelieving friend, coworker, person in my daily life,

I had an epiphany today. It sounds like a religious term, but I'm sure people who don't follow Jesus also have epiphanies. In fact, I searched the word on the Internet, and I'm right on both counts. An epiphany can mean a Christian festival commemorating the appearance of Christ to the Gentiles. That's the religious term and not what happened to me today. An epiphany can also be a sudden, intuitive perception or insight usually sparked by something commonplace. That's what happened to me today and what I'm sure could happen to you, too. (Although Jesus might reach out to you. You might respond. Which would be cool because then you would have both kinds of epiphanies, but I digress.)

Anyway, it happened as I sat around a conference table at work only half-listening to the presenter. As I glanced at the other meeting attendees, I realized something that bothered me. It occurred to me that I didn't love these people. Not any of them.

I liked them. They were nice enough. I didn't wish any of them harm, but I wasn't losing sleep over their eternal destinations. I saw them at work. I interacted with them at work. I left them at work. Done.

I follow Jesus. I'm heading to heaven. The people close to me are going to heaven. Apparently, I'm good with leaving it at that. That's not good.

The epiphany followed me through the day. *Hello, coffee barista. I don't love you. Hey there, client—nope, no love for you either. Checkout clerk at the pharmacy*

I visit every few days? No. I don't love you. Neighbor with whom I share daily pleasantries? Not an inkling of love for you at all.

In the past, I would have spent this day knocking my ability to witness, perusing books on evangelism, and even researching local workshops on sharing my faith. I might have prayed for boldness, courage, or confidence. Today, though, because of the epiphany, I saw the root of my problem. It's a crisis of love.

I've made sure the people I love know the truth of Jesus Christ: my kids, parents, husband, and closest friends. My inner circle. My readers. My love for these is so great I ignore fear. I walk through fire to make sure they know the truth of Jesus Christ. Moreover, I'm not satisfied with their just "getting the gospel." Oh no, I pray for and seek every opportunity to encourage them to go deeper with Jesus. That's what I do for the people I love.

Not you people. I'm apparently completely at peace having no concern over your eternal outcome. You don't know Jesus? You're destined to be separated from God forever? Whatever. Man, that's cold. I am cold. Without love. Not a pretty picture. That was my epiphany.

My love isn't enough. I cannot serve as your ambassador to Jesus on my faulted, human love alone. That's why my evangelism runs on fumes. It's not for lack of skills; it's for lack of love. It's the result of an empty love tank. It's a love lapse.

If I loved you, I would rock as your missionary. If I loved you, I'd scale the mountain of my fear, insecurity, and lack of confidence to tell you about Jesus. If I loved you, my love would build a bridge to your heart, and the gospel would roll like a tank across that bridge to breach your walls. Oh yeah, if I loved you, you'd be hearing about Jesus.

Today, I prayed a new prayer: "Lord, fill me with your love for the people in my life. My love is a pathetic counterfeit. My love pales. My love is afraid of its own shadow. Give me your love. Let your love loosen my tongue and free me to witness from a place of strength—the launch pad of your great heart. In Jesus's name, amen."

You don't know Jesus, but you may want to pray, too. Jesus is the only way to eternal life. If you lived in some other country, there would be loving missionaries devoted to communicating that truth to you. You? You're stuck with me. It's not looking too good for you, my friend.

Fortunately for both of us, today I had an epiphany and prayed that prayer. Watch out now, because God's love is coming after us both and his love never gives up.

Love (well, asking Jesus for love and expecting him to answer),
Me

Small Steps Toward Slaying Giants

1. First John 4:13-21 provides a basis for understanding the relationship between loving others and loving God. How does loving someone free us from fear? How can this revolutionize our approach to sharing our faith?
2. List people in your life who don't know Jesus and pray daily for Jesus to give you his love for them.

❧ ❧ ❧

One Stone for Your Sling: That's why my evangelism runs on fumes. It's not for lack of skills; it's for lack of love. It's the result of an empty love tank. It's a love lapse.

Brotherly Affection

Day Three

Confessions of a Second-Class Christian

Brotherly Affection Begins at Home

Recently I visited a place that reminded me that I don't really belong in the family of God. You know, because the people there know my stuff. Some people have met me through my writing and others through work. Some have become friends through common circumstances, but these church people from my long-ago past had known me in failure, pain, rumors, and lies. In their minds, that cancels me out from fully belonging to the family.

You know how it works, don't you? I can sit with them because Jesus even let in prostitutes and tax collectors, but I'll never really be one of them. I can worship alongside them, but only from the cheap seats.

When I was a child, I read a Christmas story called "The Little Match Girl" by Hans Christian Anderson—a story much more tragic than my own. It's about a homeless girl lighting magical matches on New Year's Eve so she can see Christmas tableaus inside people's homes she cannot enter. With her last match, she sees her grandmother who has gone on to heaven, beckoning her there to a beautiful place where she is welcome at last.

That story touched me because back then I imagined most people had perfect families like the ones the girl saw through the walls. I hoped that if I was perfect, I could overcome my own imperfect origin. Then, if I could create a perfect family with Jesus's help, I would belong.

But you know there's no perfection on this side of glory, even when we know Jesus. The moment we learn that lesson, when we light our final match and find ourselves still sitting out in the cold, it can shatter our faith. Really, what shatters is the illusion of faith, and that's where true faith begins.

Until that moment, many of us believe our entrance into God's kingdom is some kind of partnership between Jesus and us. We know Jesus does *most* of the work, but we function under the delusion it's something of a 60/40 proposition—70/30 at the most. This gives us, we believe, the right to look down on those for whom it seems a 90/10 kind of deal.

But when we light our last match and it fails to save us from the cold reality of our world, when we fail God, when we fall in a way that's undeniable, that's when we realize salvation is 100 percent Jesus. Our entrance to his kingdom rests solely on his shoulders on the cross. He fully redeemed us with no help from us even if we've grown up in the church since cradle roll. Maybe that's why the Holy Spirit initially arrived with "tongues of fire" (Acts 2:3 ESV). We'd spent all our matches and couldn't even muster a spark without Jesus.

Matthew understood being an outsider. He didn't belong anywhere. He didn't belong with his people, the Jews, because he'd sold them out to work for their oppressors, the Romans. He didn't belong with the Romans because by birth, he was a Jew. He is, for me, evidence that the disciples didn't invent a religion, because they never would have included Matthew. He didn't belong.

Yet Jesus chose him. Loved him. Included him in his inner circle. Commissioned him. Redeemed him completely. Selected him to write one of only four Gospels—words that millions would read and reread for centuries. Jesus took the outsider and made him the ultimate inside man.

None of us would have seen anything worth redeeming about Matthew. He stole. He lied. He betrayed his own people. He cooperated with the enemy. He was a lowlife. We wouldn't have seen anything worth redeeming about Matthew because he became of worth through his redemption in Christ. I wasn't worth redeeming either, but I now have worth because he redeemed me.

The enemy knows we feel like second-class Christians. He plays on that. He sticks his finger in that wound and orchestrates circumstances to rip it wide open again. His intent is to paralyze, to immobilize, and to render us impotent in the work of furthering God's kingdom—if he can. We need to spot his attack and guard against it. Our defense is God's Word—a steady assault of the truth that he calls us to belong, as Paul says in Romans 1:6, including "you who are called by Jesus Christ." Our defense is Christ himself. He chose to redeem us, to include us, to bring us into his family, and let no one speak against his work.

Have you ever felt like a second-class Christian because of your failings, people's false impressions of you, or through the failings of loved ones? Resist the enemy's attempts to contain the work of Christ in you and through you by muting your gifts, which are for the building up of the body of Christ. Because, you see, even this work of inclusion isn't about any one of us; it's about Jesus and about building the church of which he is the head.

No matter what our circumstances, the truth of them, or what others think about them, Jesus has the final word on our lives. That word is *redeemed.*

Small Steps Toward Slaying Giants

1. First Peter 2:1-12 explains how we are to act toward one another and how we, as a church, should think about one another and why. How does it say to behave? How does it say to think about ourselves? Why?
2. Galatians 6:1-10 sheds more light on how to treat one another in the church or within our faith communities. How would it help you topple the giants in your life to have others treat you this way?

One Stone for Your Sling: Our defense is God's Word—a steady assault of the truth that God calls us to belong to the family of God.

Brotherly Affection

Day Four

Jesus Loves Martha

Brotherly Affection That Cares to Confront

If there is now no condemnation in Jesus Christ, then we all owe Martha a huge apology.

Martha was a real woman. A Jesus-lover who welcomed him and his followers into her home. She took care of her household—her brother, Lazarus, and her sister, Mary. She cooked, cleaned, washed, tended, and fed; and when someone died, she prepared the body as she mourned.

I imagine Martha had seen death up close and mourned often in her life. There's no mention of living parents, spouses, or children. In ancient Israel, three siblings didn't choose to share a home unless other options hadn't opened up for them.

I imagine Martha was a serious, no-nonsense woman. On one busy day in her household, when the demands of caring for everyone got to her, she asked Jesus to nudge Mary into helping her. Jesus redirected Martha's attention from fussing over everything to paying attention to Him. It was an important moment in Martha's life. But it was just a moment.

It was an important lesson for all of us, but it was only one lesson we must learn. Now, due to the branding machine of modern life, poor Martha has become a watchword for everything a Christian woman shouldn't be as we all strive to be like Mary.

On one level this is okay because we should pay attention to Jesus as Mary did. We shouldn't fuss around about earthly matters to the exclusion of spending time with Jesus the way Martha did. Still, Martha wasn't a character in a story designed to be the biblical equivalent of Goofus to Mary's Gallant.

Martha was a woman like me and other women I know, trying to do those things that please God and serve those she loved even when she was tired and life was hard. She was a woman trying to get it right and loving those around her the best way she knew how. Jesus wasn't condemning Martha with his redirection; he was freeing her because he loved her. He didn't want her to become Mary; he wanted her to be a Martha who paid attention to him.

Women I know condemn the Martha in themselves. They work hard caring for those around them, preparing delicious food and delightful tables. Unfortunately, then they scold themselves and think themselves displeasing to God because they get irritable or tired in the process. That's not what the whole Mary and Martha thing was about.

In her whole life, Martha had likely seen her worth only in what she could do and provide for others. It's why she was seeing Mary's contribution to the day as useless. Jesus was telling her, not that he condemned her efforts, but that he saw *her*. He valued her, not for her roasted lamb and her perfect lentil stew, but because he knew her heart and wanted her to know his.

John 11:5 says, "Jesus loved Martha." And he did. It's funny that I don't see many books written about the conversation they had when Lazarus had died. "When Martha heard that Jesus was coming, she went to meet him, but Mary remained in the house. Martha said to Jesus, 'Lord, if you had been here, my brother wouldn't have died. Even now I know that whatever you ask God, God will give you'" (John 11:20-22).

Do you hear Martha's complete faith in Jesus? Do you see how she went out to him even in her sorrow? She cares enough to confront him for his delay in coming.

"Jesus told her, 'Your brother will rise again.' Martha replied, 'I know that he will rise in the resurrection on the last day.' Jesus said to her, 'I am the resurrection and the life. Whoever believes in me will live, even though they die. Everyone who lives and believes in me will never die. Do you believe this?'" (John 11:23-26). Here Jesus speaks the words to Martha that reveal who he is and why he came. They are friends, and he tells her what he's about in this world.

"She replied, 'Yes, Lord, I believe that you are the Christ, God's Son, the one who is coming into the world'" (John 11:27).

Martha believed Jesus and put her faith in him.

Consider this. Lazarus, her brother, was dead. There's much to do when the head of your household dies. There are details to which someone must attend. There are also traditions, protocols, and mourners who need food. Martha left all those to go out to meet Jesus.

She took his redirection and moved into a deeper relationship with him. We miss this because we like to flatten Bible people and stick them up on a flannel board so we don't have to let them affect our daily lives.

I want to be like Mary *and* Martha. They were real women, complex and amazing, with real-life stories. They had real friendships with Jesus. They loved him, served him, worshiped him, and challenged him. He enjoyed them, corrected them, and loved them. He never condemned them or made them feel they were worthless. He would hate for us to take this story about Martha and turn it on ourselves as a whipping stick.

In hundreds of Christian homes, loving, diligent hands prepare meals, oversee lessons or homework, work hard to provide, help with projects, and create beautiful, comfortable spaces. These hardworking hands belong to women paying attention to Jesus. They aren't Marthas or Marys, and they don't hang out on flannel boards. Sometimes they get caught up on the wrong things, but they can repent, turn around, and run out to meet Jesus anytime.

Don't listen if Satan tries to mumble some Martha condemnation into your ear when you've gotten tired and a little snarky. Turn to Jesus and give him your attention. He'll remind you that you're loved, noticed, valued, cherished, redeemed.

He blesses you, Martha, and he loves you. Run to Jesus. He doesn't condemn you. He's freed you!

Small Steps Toward Slaying Giants

1. Read Proverbs 27:6 and think about a time another Christian told you a hard truth that helped you grow deeper with Jesus. Were you able to thank that brother or sister? Even if you've done it before, encourage that person by thanking him or her again today.
2. Do you spend time criticizing yourself or thinking harsh thoughts even though you're working to please the Lord and serve others? Read Romans 8 every day this week and commit to memory the first two verses.

One Stone for Your Sling: Jesus didn't want Martha to become Mary; he wanted her to be a Martha who paid attention to him.

Brotherly Affection

Day Five

Other Christians Make Me Wonder

Brotherly Affection That Unites

Other Christians really make me wonder.

For example, I wonder if in the Central African Republic, following a massacre by terrorists on the people's church grounds, when they gathered for worship, dirt from thirty freshly dug graves beneath their fingernails, ears still ringing from the gun blasts ricocheting off their sanctuary walls, did they complain because the service ran long? Or did they read from Habakkuk with insight that I pray I'll never gain?[2]

I wonder about a mother in chains in Sudan. As she sat nursing her newborn and praying for the strength not to renounce her faith, her toddler languishing beside her in prison, did she refuse to hear a message by a visiting preacher because he was covering material that she already knew or that wasn't delivered in an engaging fashion? As her husband gathered with other believers, I wonder if he complained about the style of song they sang as they poured out their hearts to God. Or did they read from Lamentations 3 with a depth of understanding I don't envy?[3]

In Gorea, Cameroon, where the voices of all the Christians have been silenced, I wonder if somewhere in the world, someone remembered to pray for those souls residing there who still need a witness to the truth of Jesus Christ. Did someone intercede for those who murdered our brothers and sisters there, for those who betrayed, for those walking dead who have snuffed the only lights that shone in their darkness?[4]

Will they pray for a fulfillment of Luke 19:40? When the rocks and stones cry out around the people of Gorea, will the people then repent and turn to the living God?

I wonder if in China, when the wife of a Christian bookstore employee imprisoned for engaging in his trade gathered with other believers to pray, did she share testimony about how God found her a parking space close to the store that week? Did those gathered pass over the offering even though Wenxi Li's family relies on their gifts while he remains imprisoned for his crime? When he shared the gospel with other captives behind those barred doors, did he water down the truth so the other prisoners would like him?[5]

Or did their call to worship include verses from Corinthians that they've memorized without effort because those words are their life?

> We are experiencing all kinds of trouble, but we aren't crushed. We are confused, but we aren't depressed. We are harassed, but we aren't abandoned. We are knocked down, but we aren't knocked out!
>
> We always carry Jesus' death around in our bodies so that Jesus' life can also be seen in our bodies. We who are alive are always being handed over to death for Jesus' sake so that Jesus' life can also be seen in our bodies that are dying. So death is at work in us, but life is at work in you. (2 Corinthians 4:8-12)

And I wonder if, in North Korea, when my brothers and sisters gather for worship, do they worry about what the others are wearing or complain about the pastor's tie? Does their pastor live, or will they share their memories of messages delivered before guards took him from them? Will they weep? Will they wonder if anyone remembers them or knows their suffering? When the call to worship comes, will they choose to sleep in, to forgo gathering and instead wash their cars or mow their lawns, or will they wait for corporate worship like a man crossing a desert waits for signs of water?[6]

When they read from 2 Timothy 3:1-5, will they know Jesus understands the times in which they live?

> But mark this: There will be terrible times in the last days. People will be lovers of themselves, lovers of money, boastful, proud, abusive, disobedient to their parents, ungrateful, unholy, without love, unforgiving, slanderous,

> without self-control, brutal, not lovers of the good, treacherous, rash, conceited, lovers of pleasure rather than lovers of God—having a form of godliness but denying its power. Have nothing to do with such people. (NIV)

I also wonder about us in the West, if we think God created these brothers and sisters who suffer and die to be object lessons in our sermons or if we here will enjoy our freedom on this outpost of glory indefinitely.

I wonder, will some of us get that we are called to serve those who suffer, that they are one with us and when they suffer, so do we, whether we acknowledge it or not? Will we serve them through prayerful warfare, through lament, by being their voices while cruel hands choke theirs? Will we worship like those who know gathering together to focus on our Lord is a privilege, a joy, a gift, and as necessary as the blood in our veins?

Will we honor those whose lives are taken from them by spending our freedom, not on ourselves, but on Jesus? And when we read from Revelation 3:1-6, will we see ourselves or know that is who we might have been if we hadn't heeded the call of the Spirit?

Other Christians make me wonder. They make me wonder how they hold on. They make me wonder at their courage, their willingness to sacrifice, and the depth of their relationship with Jesus Christ. They make me wonder how I can better serve them and Jesus. They make me wonder how long my own freedom will last. One day, will I wonder why I didn't maximize it when I had it?

Do other Christians make you wonder, too?

Small Steps Toward Slaying Giants

1. What is God saying in 1 Corinthians 12:21-26 about our connection to believers around the world? What is he saying about our relationship to the entire body of Christ? What does this mean to you?
2. What are ways you can stand with those who suffer in parts of the world where persecution of Christians is rampant? How can you pray? Are there ways you can serve them? Prayerfully consider this for yourself and discuss it, too, with your congregation or small group.

One Stone for Your Sling: Will we honor those whose lives are taken from them by spending our freedom, not on ourselves, but on Jesus?

Brotherly Affection

Day Six

Pray, Reflect, Process, Pray

Ask God to direct you to activities that will give you brotherly affection in increasing measure. Try inviting two or three people from your church out for coffee. Choose people either much younger or much older than you are. Show a genuine interest in their Christian experience and do a lot of listening.

Reflect on what you've read in his Word this week. Go back to passages that spoke to where you are right now or inspired you to growth. Reread and reflect.

Actively engage in a preferred activity that helps you process what God has said to you about brotherly affection. Ask God to continue the work of building your brotherly affection in increasing measure. Now, lather, rinse, repeat.

16

Love That Invites and Incites

Love

Day One

Nobody loves me."

The little boy, preschool age, looked at the cracked tiles on his kitchen floor as he spoke, swinging feet that didn't reach the floor from the dining table chair.

"I care about you," I replied.

"You get paid to care about me," he answered. (I work with families in crisis.) Then looking into my eyes, he said, "I want someone to love me for nuthin'. Do you get that?"

Yeah, I nodded. I get that. Love for no reason. Love when there's nothing in it for you. Love because I'm worthy of love. Love for nuthin'.

The cries of a billion young hearts. Children and teens who sit at kitchen tables piled high with junk mail, collection notices, applications for assistance, summons from court, everything but warm food or a clean space for homework or a game of Go Fish.

Tough Times for Love

In the days when Jesus walked the earth, the children of Israel suffered from bitter oppression beneath the heavy boot of Roman rule. Beneath the taxation and corruption of their own people who sold them out for silver. Beneath the unjust, loveless, religious rule of men who loved full bellies and flattery more than they loved the God they represented to poor carpenters and shepherds paying pennies for pigeons to sacrifice for their common sins.

Evil was systemic. Corruption epidemic. Despair rampant. Still, God's answer wasn't an army, a coup, a political takeover, or a flood. He didn't create a program, a system of care, or a political party.

His answer was a man. One man who came and loved us. He loved us—face to face, hand to wound, eye to eye, belly to the table, sitting-and-sweating-with-us close. He loved with words. With actions. With truth. He loved large. He loved small. Out of love for the Father and for us, he died to himself every minute of every day.

Hands-on God. Personal-relationship God. One-soul-at-a-time God. You-matter-because-you-were-my-idea God. When the Pharisees tried to trick him into instituting policy, he told them a story about a man they would hate, a Samaritan. This Samaritan found a stranger, robbed and beaten in a ditch, and went out of his way to tend his wounds and provide for his care—personal attention, inconvenient and costly individual treatment. Love in motion.

Love in Motion

"Love your neighbor," Jesus proclaimed, is the second greatest command. Love God. Love others. Heaven celebrates when a program instituted by someone on earth provides care and comfort to thousands of needy people. But I believe there are bells, songs, roaring laughter, and parties when one individual walks next door and offers to mow the elderly neighbor's yard. Or plays catch with the son of the single mom from the small group. Or brings coffee and a car fan belt to the man who lost his job.

Programs and ministries do good things for people. Professions, politics, and biblical policies are important in moving forward the work of Christ on earth. Still, nothing demonstrates the love of Jesus to someone better than loving him or her for nuthin'. Face-to-face. Ball-to-glove. Coffee-mug-to-long story. Open-heart-to-wounded-heart. Game of Go Fish, let-me-check-your-homework love.

Draining Love

Pharisees love the keep-clean, hands-off, systematic, programmatic delegation of love. Love distributed neatly through proper channels. Jesus lived an interrupt-your-day, break-into-your-agenda, and stop-the-presses-for-a-stranger kind of love.

Love that was in the way and out of the way. Love that found a way and showed the way. Love that was dirty at the end of the day. Love that got sweat and blood on it. Love that was in your face and out of the box. Love that touched the loved one in a way that he felt the power drain from him when it happened.

When was the last time you felt the power drain from you from loving someone?

Love is one of those qualities we think we understand until God calls us to do it at significant cost. We're so accustomed to the word we've diluted it of its potency. When we see it lived out sacrificially—first responders swarming into the Twin Towers, an elderly husband carrying his failing wife to bed each night, a pregnant woman delaying cancer treatments until her child is born—it reminds us we've barely scratched the surface of love.

We've learned about love all our Christian lives. We know the Greek word Peter uses in 2 Peter 1:7 is *agape*. With the click of a finger, we can locate dozens of sermons or podcasts teaching us why that word is special, significant, and elevated above other forms of love. We've read and heard it all.

We don't deliver it to those who need it by talking about it. We deliver it by living it. I suspect when Jesus met daily with his Father, our God wasn't handing him a daily to-do list as much as discussing his daily "to-love" list. Walking through the Gospels is a discipleship course in love.

Love Lessons for Life

Love tells the truth. Love does what God tells it to do. Love is patient with interruptions. Love invests in people. Love is free, unhurried, and unworried about basic needs. Love crosses boundaries. Love tells stories, weeps, laughs, corrects, and heals. Love is prepared to die.

Love isn't something we study one Sunday or one semester in a small group and then move on. Love is our whole agenda. We can get everything else right, but if we miss love, we miss it all. The other beans we bury are meaningless if we don't unleash the power in the one called love.

Every giant toppled in Scripture was felled because someone allowed the love of the Lord to cast out all other fears. The enemy knows the power of love and so has waged a full-out assault on love in our times. This is why Jesus warned us of the times to come and what would happen to love:

> They will arrest you, abuse you, and they will kill you. All nations will hate you on account of my name. At that time many will fall away. They will betray each other and hate each other. Many false prophets will appear and deceive many people. Because disobedience will expand, the love of many will grow cold. But the one who endures to the end will be delivered. This gospel of the kingdom will be proclaimed throughout the world as a testimony to all the nations. Then the end will come. (Matthew 24:9-14)

Love is our aim. It deserves our full attention, effort, and strength. "Let us consider each other carefully for the purpose of sparking love and good deeds. Don't stop meeting together with other believers, which some people have gotten into the habit of doing. Instead, encourage each other, especially as you see the day drawing near" (Hebrews 10:24-25).

Word Study Exercise

Read 1 Corinthians 13 and make a list of people you love. Think about each one and ask yourself if you offer them the love described in 1 Corinthians 13:4-7.

Read 1 John 4:7-21. Consider the list of giants you made at the start of this book. What does love look like in the face of those giants? How can God's perfect love cast fear out of those circumstances? In light of this passage, what should we consider before we casually state we love God but don't love his church?

Biblical Role Model Ministudy

Jesus is love. He is a living, breathing study in love. If we want to know what love looks like in the flesh, we have only to look to Jesus. Read one of the Gospels (Matthew, Mark, Luke, or John) in one sitting. As you read, make a list of the action verbs ascribed to Jesus. What can they tell us about how love acts? Read a separate gospel each week for four weeks and do the same each time. How does Jesus exemplify love?

Heritage of Faith Walkers

Keith Green lived his love. Keith was a Jewish convert to Christ, a singer and songwriter who was killed in a 1982 plane crash with two of his four children. Keith and his wife, Melody, practiced extensive hospitality, ministering out of their home to recovering drug addicts and prostitutes, the homeless, and single pregnant women, eventually founding Last Days Ministries.

Other believers known for their love are Desmond Mpilo Tutu, Dr. Paul Wilson Brand, Catherine of Siena, Sojourner Truth, and Jim Wallis. Many of the finest examples of sacrificial love aren't famous. They love quietly in your congregation, neighborhood, or extended family. Consider one of them today and let that person know you see and appreciate the love he or she demonstrates in Jesus's name.

Small Steps Toward Slaying Giants

1. Do you know what makes the people in your immediate circle feel loved? Love them that way today. Don't know the answer? Ask them.
2. For one week, forego your daily to-do list for a daily to-love list. How does that affect your thinking, your actions, and your feelings about your day?

One Stone for Your Sling: When was the last time you felt the power drain from you from loving someone?

Love

Day Two

When You Say You Love My Daughter

Love That Promises to Last

When you say you love my daughter…

I think about all the ways she has been loved up until now.

She was loved before she was conceived, before time began, by a God who imagined a smart, quirky, spiritual girl. A girl who loves to be active, writes with her own unique voice, and holds back until she really knows someone but then gives her fierce loyalty.

A girl who is only beginning to understand and unlock her own potential. A lover of words, coffee, Stephen King novels, Ted Dekker, T. S. Eliot, peanut butter, country music, and Dr. Seuss. A girl who's had her challenges and faced them like a gladiator. A girl who's become a woman gifted at working with children, with words, and with a quick answer. A woman who loves the Lord who created her and pours her heart into a worship that spills over into her day.

He has loved her since before time began—enough to create her, enough to redeem her with his own Son, enough to claim her as a Jesus follower when she was still a child. He loves her unconditionally, passionately, and practically. He loves her sacrificially. He loves her eternally. This is what she knows of love.

She's been loved by her father and me since before she was conceived. We dreamed about her, longed for her, and welcomed her without reservation. Her brother pronounced her our family's "happy ending," but her arrival was only the beginning of our love adventure.

We've loved her with truth, with biblical teaching and modeling, with gentle correction and direction, and with honest praise. We've loved her with a safe home, warm food, clothes, education, companionship, and community.

We've loved her imperfectly but consistently with patience, forgiveness, soft words, firm boundaries, and our own lives.

We love her enough to encourage and exhort her to be her best self. We love her enough to protect her but also to trust her to the Lord when she faces trials that occur for the refining of her character and faith. We, too, will love her forever. We love her stubbornly, infuriatingly, persistently, and sacrificially. This is what she knows of love from us.

Her grandparents love her lavishly, generously, hilariously, unconditionally, and protectively. They love her sacrificially, and their love for her will extend long beyond their years, echoing through her life to the next generations. Her brother loves her offhandedly, as brothers do, but loyally, protectively, and faithfully. Her aunts and uncles love her joyfully, securely, and protectively as well. This is what she knows of love from them.

So, when you tell me you love my daughter, this is what I hear you saying. I understand you to mean you're willing to pick up the baton of love we pass to you in the way we've defined love for her until this day. And when you say you love my daughter, I understand you to say you already know the love she's known from our Father God. You're ready to be included in the love she has known from us and the others who have loved her to this time. You're ready to love her solely, practically, wholly, patiently, faithfully, joyfully, stubbornly, protectively, sacrificially, and forever.

This is what she has known of love, so if you tell her you love her, this is what she understands you're saying. When she says she loves you back, this is the love she's offering. We all love imperfectly this side of glory, but within the power and grace of a relationship with Jesus Christ, we can love as he does.

So if, when you say you love my daughter, this is what you're saying, welcome to our lives, young man. We've prayed for you and waited to love you since before you were born, too.

Small Steps Toward Slaying Giants

1. We start out intensely focused on loving our immediate loved ones, but life has a way of settling so we take them for granted. Look at your loved ones today and list what you love about them. Show them the list.
2. Read Song of Solomon 8:6-7. How does this image of love differ from the one presented by the world? How is love strong?

❧ ❧ ❧

One Stone for Your Sling: When you say you love my daughter, I understand you to mean you are willing to pick up the baton of love we pass to you in the way we have defined love for her until this day.

Love

Day Three

I Have Been Marked as a Hater

Speaking Truth in Love

I went to bed one night a loving person but woke up a representative of hate. What happened, you ask? It is time we asked, isn't it, because it happened to you, too.

The teenage boy in my Sunday school class brought a newspaper photo into class. The day before, there had been a gay pride parade in a nearby city. The photo was of one of the more exuberant floats passing a group of scowling protesters who held signs proclaiming that God hates gays. Pointing to the photo, the young man said, "I don't get it. Which side are we on?"

A tenth-grade girl in the class asked if we could chat privately. "Mrs. Roeleveld, I'm worried I'm not really a Christian."

"What's causing you to doubt?" I asked.

"I love all the wrong people at school. I don't feel as though I can hate anybody."

These teens were absorbing the deception that Satan set off like a bug fogger on this generation. They actually believe Christians are haters, that the world sets the best standard for love. They believe that we have to choose between truth and love; ergo, those who dare to speak unpleasant truths are filled with hate.

And where are we, the church? Backing down. Retreating. Staying silent. Watching evil abscond with love. Inhaling fumes from the getaway car. Knowing truth cannot be compromised, we assume love can be; so we turn it over to Satan without a fight, making Christians who speak the most about love suspect.

We do not have to choose between truth and love. Jesus never did, and his Spirit lives within us. Why have we believed this lie?

As my father gets older, he has more to say to those of us he loves. He feels the press of time. His conversations are urgent—full of what he feels is important to impart. Jesus felt this on the night he was betrayed. More than this, he *knew* the time of his death was drawing near. In his last precious hours with his disciples, what was the theme of his conversation?

> Little children, I'm with you for a little while longer. You will look for me—but, just as I told the Jewish leaders, I also tell you now—"Where I'm going, you can't come."
>
> I give you a new commandment: Love each other. Just as I have loved you, so you also must love each other. This is how everyone will know that you are my disciples, when you love each other. (John 13:33-35)

He doesn't say, "All people will know you're my disciples because you'll turn out to be right." He doesn't say, "All people will know you're my disciples because you won't compromise on what's correct." He does say, "All people will know you're my disciples if you have love for one another."

Love is our *shibboleth*.[1] Our password. Our uniform. Our code. When we allowed it to be hijacked without pursuit, we messed up big time. Now the next generation of young people believe they can't be Christians if they can't find it within themselves to hate.

We must wage a recovery mission for love. We should be hosting conferences and workshops on how to love. Our pulpits and airwaves should blare messages with the instructions to love. Love discussions should fill our small groups, and we should have weekly love check-ins. How are you loving God? Your neighbor? Your enemies? What creative ways have you found to express love to your coworkers? Your church family? Your unsaved loved ones?

We should have love seminars. Christian artists, musicians, filmmakers, writers, and choreographers should collaborate on vehicles for the message of love—love, which is the greatest, hardest, least compromisable truth of all truths.

If they will know we are his disciples by our love and we let that be stolen and counterfeited, how will they see him in us, find him, and open to his love for them? Every generation has a mission in furthering His kingdom. Could ours be to recover love?

Small Steps Toward Slaying Giants

1. Read Ephesians 4:1-16. This passage contains the phrase "speaking the truth with love" (v. 15). Set in context, what is the point of speaking the truth in love? Where is it best practiced? Have you experienced the benefit of others speaking the truth to you with love?
2. Look back at your daily to-love list from day one. Is there anyone on that list who needs the truth spoken in love? Pray for guidance and then send him or her a note or an invitation for coffee.

❧ ❧ ❧

One Stone for Your Sling: Love is our *shibboleth*. Our password. Our uniform. Our code. When we allowed it to be hijacked without pursuit, we messed up big time.

Love

❧ Day Four ❧

Don't Make Me Pull This Book Over!

Corrective Love

My young son accused me of being a "Klingon mom."

Klingons are a warrior race on *Star Trek: The Next Generation*. Zack meant it as an insult. I wore it as a badge of honor.

Initially I wasn't good at *skillfully* loving my firstborn. I loved him and enjoyed receiving his love in return, so much so I would back off discipline and not set the clear boundaries a child needs. God graciously enlightened me, however, the day my toddler asked his father and me a serious question from the back seat of the car: "How come you guys never bow down to me?" Clearly, a Gibbs-slap[2] from God. I was doing something seriously wrong.

I learned because God is a good parent. By watching him, I matured in my understanding of love. My initial love for my son was immature and selfish. I soaked in the affection he had for me, but because I was insecure about losing the return on my love investment, I backed off from risking it, even for short periods of discipline. That changed.

Fast forward two years. My little guy saw a package of stickers at the grocery store and *wanted* them. I said no. He pushed me with both hands and insisted, "Yes!" That shove not only ended our shopping trip but also lost him every toy in his room. That afternoon, we boxed up each action figure, stuffed animal, and Lego. He was allowed to earn back one small box at a time until he learned to appreciate what he had and not imagine he was entitled to more on demand.

"I don't like you!" he shouted mid-process. "You're like a Klingon mom! I'm gonna go live with another mom. A mom who really loves me."

It's not fun when your child doesn't like you. It's frustrating when he questions your love because you've set a line, stuck to your guns, or haven't yielded to a demand. But here is a true statement that may sound downright revolutionary in this day and age: children do not know how to love.

Children are born with the capacity to love, but we must teach them about love as they grow just as we teach them about all other aspects of life. Toddlers believe love is someone giving them everything they want when, actually, love gives them what they need while teaching them to want the right things.

Daily I see the result of parents who offer their children only an immature, selfish love. Years ago, one father had young children who were so unruly no one liked them—not even him. We sat with a state worker who said, "Do you realize, sir, I'm going to remove your children from your custody if you can't get them in hand?"

The dad hung his head. "I can't be tough on them. I love them too much."

The worker continued, "You've allowed them to reach a point where no one wants to be around them. Not even you. They've become mentally unhealthy and dangerous to others, and they're only in elementary school. Are you willing to work with someone to teach them to behave, or will I have to remove them from your care?"

He wouldn't look us in the eyes as he said, "Take them."

That's not love. Not the mature, healthy, full-grown love a child needs and deserves.

Too many of us expect God to love us the way this father "loved" his children: giving us everything we want, turning a blind eye to our failings, repeating warning after warning about behavior but never following through with consequences.

Like spiritual toddlers, we also want to receive this kind of love from one another: "I can't be with Christians who don't accept everything about me"; "I can't worship with people who talk about hell, sin, or right and wrong"; "Jesus was all about love. I want to be with people who love others and forget all this nonsense about sin."

My son thought he knew what love was. To him, love was my yielding to his wishes and letting him act the way he felt like acting. There were times when he, in his immaturity, withheld his affection from me to "teach me a lesson." I learned to endure those times for his sake. The love I learned to offer him was a love willing to suffer—to make him uncomfortable for his own good. It was love with a spine. A love that can survive in a crazy world. A strong love he knows will be there for him always.

He knows I love and accept him, but he also knows I don't accept behavior that is beneath him. Neither does Jesus. Our Lord expects us to grow into behavior that reflects our new nature.

Jesus was clear that he didn't come to abolish the law but that he came to fulfill it. In the Sermon on the Mount (Matthew 5–7), he essentially tells his listeners that Moses went easy on them! Moses told them not to murder, but Jesus told them if they're angry with their brother, they're already guilty. Moses told them not to commit adultery, but Jesus said if they lust after a woman, they're already in sin. There was nothing accepting or inclusive about his statements. He died for us, but he demonstrated redemptive love, not love that looks the other way.

Whenever I blog about love, I receive private messages from readers worried that because I'm writing about love, I may be ready to waver on biblical truth. Clearly we, as a church family, need to have a conversation about love. Love tells the truth. Love sets boundaries. Love is fierce, strong, powerful, and redemptive. Love doesn't indulge or give its children away with no good reason. Love stays and does the hard work of raising them.

It's easy to talk tough about the call to love our enemies, but if we can't love the person in the next pew, maybe we're clinging to a lesser love than the one to which we've been called. How will you love a terrorist when you can't love that uptight lady who scowls or that awkward teen who smacks her gum?

Love is our thing, people! God is love. Love comes from God. Love is his idea. Let's act on this and recover love from the hands of darkness. To know God is to know love. Why aren't we the go-to experts on love?

Does the topic of love make you nervous? Pay attention to that. Love—true love—is downright unsettling. What does that say about where we are as a church if it's controversial to talk about love? We all need to have this conversation—now. Anyone else want to pull over and chat?

Small Steps Toward Slaying Giants

1. Why do we feel the need to choose between love and truth? Have a conversation with others in your faith community about it. List passages in which Jesus told the truth and loved simultaneously.
2. Look over the list of giants you created. Can loving with truth topple any of those giants? What difference could love and truth make in facing them?

One Stone for Your Sling: Love—true love—is downright unsettling.

Love

Day Five

The Day the Church Grew Bored with Love

Freeing Love

Have you ever been snagged in your own follies?

I arrived early for worship one week, and the music team invited me to join them. It had been a while since I sang with a praise team, so I agreed. As we sang the first song, I put my hand behind my back. When I went to raise it in praise, my bracelet snagged on my sweater. There I stood, worshiping before the congregation, handcuffed to myself.

Trying not to panic and to continue to sing the actual words, I kept the front of myself as still as possible while behind my back, I wriggled, twisted, and yanked in a song-length attempt to extricate myself from myself. There you have it, loved ones, my spiritual life in a nutshell.

We all get snagged on ourselves, and it frustrates us not only during worship but also throughout our days as we maneuver around our self-imposed incapacitation, trying still to keep our eyes on God. One way we get tangled up is by ignoring love.

Stop. Ask yourself how you reacted when I mentioned love again. Were you a little disappointed because I'm still harping on this subject? Are you anticipating you won't learn anything in the next lines because you have the love thing in hand? You might think the rest of this chapter is going to be nonspecific fluff with no takeaway, like what you've heard a million times on the topic of love, right?

The day Christians became bored with love, the day we stopped being students of love, the day we relegated love to the greeting-card aisle at CVS and Nicholas Sparks films, is the day we snagged ourselves on ourselves and wondered where our freedom went.

I heard a preacher once say, "Well, this passage is about love, and there are only so many sermons one can preach about love, so I pulled out an old one." What? Kudos for honesty, I guess. I've felt that way sometimes, but God's emphasis on love in his Word indicates there's more to it than we've allowed ourselves to see. There are endless facets to God's love. In fact, the apostle John makes this downright outrageous claim: "The person who doesn't love does not know God, because God is love" (1 John 4:8). If we want to know God, we must be willing to know love. If we're disciples of Christ, we're disciples of love.

With this understanding in mind, the worst thing any of us can do is to try to conjure up love from within our own hearts. We're largely unloving beings. We love those who love us. We love when there is clear reward. We love intensely—for a time. But humans are essentially love colanders. Love passes through us like rain through a leaky bucket, and we require a continual filling. We need to go to the source for love.

One of the greatest ideas that evil ever conceived was to hijack love and create sort of a Frankenstein counterfeit that was rolled out to the masses as the American free-love movements that gained unprecedented popularity in the 1960s and 1970s. God is the Creator, not Satan; but Satan can twist and mangle one of God's ideas. If he can sell enough people a pitcher full of his mock love, then they believe they've tried love and found it watery, fluffy, too sweet, and unable to hold its own beside a serving of truth.

Sort of like carob. Have you ever been given a piece of this facsimile of chocolate and told it was real chocolate? If you'd always eaten carob and were convinced it was chocolate, you might pass up a taste of the real thing even if you were sitting with a chocolatier in Paris.

Satan's campaign of pseudo-love has been wildly effective. The world now sees love as a weak thing, willing to compromise truth for sentiment. We've linked it primarily to sensuality and romance and made that the central goal of man. We actually have become so deluded by this false notion of love that some accuse the God of Scripture of being unloving! They refuse to worship a god who "doesn't know how to love."

Where are we, loved ones? The church. His bride. The recipients of his love. The vehicle for his love on this planet. We're out looking for some sexier, sturdier idea. We're sniffing the air and voicing suspicion of churches that promote love as their primary goal. We've allowed Satan to hijack love and have barely put up a fight.

It's time to take it back. It's time to reclaim love. It's time we disentangled ourselves from ourselves and became disciples of love again. The Bible says that God is love. That the greatest thing is love. That the two greatest commandments are to love. That love is stronger than death. I want me a holster full of that.

Think yourself a skilled practitioner of love? I often convince myself I'm good at it, but then I read 1 Corinthians 13:4-7, and I measure the love I offer others against that. Is the love I offer patient? Kind? Free of envy? Free of boasting? Is it humble? Does it lack rudeness? Do I insist on my own way? Am I irritable or resentful? Do I take any pleasure in wrongdoing or when others stumble? Am I always a friend to the truth? Do I offer a love that bears, believes, hopes, and endures? Do I extend a love that compels me to lay down my life for others?

A moment with God's Word and I see I'm no master practitioner in the art of love. I become aware there is more to know about love than my life shows. Lay down my life? I struggle to lay down my agenda for others, never mind my life.

For too long, we've allowed the evil one to abscond with love without a fight. How do we reclaim it? How do we learn to love so the world gets a taste of the real thing while there's still time? Let's start a conversation.

Small Steps Toward Slaying Giants

1. Read John 13–21, which tell of the last hours of Jesus' life on earth, and see if you can identify all eight of these qualities in action: faith, virtue, knowledge, self-control, steadfastness, godliness, brotherly affection, and love. What do they look like? How does that inspire you to pursue them?
2. How do you plan to increase in love in the week to come?

One Stone for Your Sling: We've allowed Satan to hijack love and have barely put up a fight.

Love

Day Six

Pray, Reflect, Process, Pray

Ask God to direct you to activities that will give you love in increasing measure. Go back to any of the suggestions at the end of this week's essays and try one you skipped, or simply decide to find a way to demonstrate love today to everyone you encounter. That could make for an interesting day!

Reflect on what you've read in his Word this week. Go back to passages that spoke to where you are right now or inspired you to growth. Reread and reflect.

Process the love passages as you create, work, play, and move. Ask God to continue the work of building your love in increasing measure. Now, lather, rinse, repeat.

Happily Ever Afterword

Ready to Face the Giants?

We still live in a land populated by giants.

We are still small.

But now we remember we come from a long line of giant-killers and that God loves small. We know we haven't been effective at toppling more giants because we've let the world tell us about our own faith, just as Jack's mother told him his beans were worthless, and because sometimes we still try to reclaim our cows.

We remember the beans contain life, life that leads to the Vine, and as we cling to the Vine (Jesus), we're filled with his Spirit. We know the eight beans aren't boring. If we cultivate them in increasing measure, we'll be effective and fruitful in our knowledge of Jesus. We know this requires effort, but we aren't afraid because we're covered by God's grace, freed in the name of Jesus to make every effort to supplement our faith.

We are ready now to face giants.

An Invitation to Continue the Conversation

I don't know about you, but I don't want our conversation to end. If you feel the same, connect with me by subscribing to my website www.loriroeleveld.com or by following the links on that page to the social media places I hang. If you'd like me to speak to your group, contact me through the website. I love to hear from readers. I care about encouraging you as you grow in the traits that will make you more effective and fruitful in your knowledge of Jesus Christ. We all have giants to topple, and we need one another's prayers and support along the way.

So come find me. I'll be looking for you.

Word and Biblical Role Model Studies for the Eight Qualities Workbook Section

Faith Word Study Exercise

Find the following Gospel passages and consider what they say about faith.

- Faith can be small: Matthew 6:30; Matthew 8:23-27
- Faith can be great: Matthew 8:5-13; Matthew 15:21-28
- Faith can be absent: Matthew 17:14-21; Mark 4:35-41
- Faith is made visible through action: Matthew 9:2; Luke 7:36-50
- Faith is active in healing: Matthew 9:1-8; Matthew 9:18-26; Matthew 9:27-31; Mark 10:46-52
- Faith can be impeded by doubt: Matthew 14:22-33; Matthew 21:18-22
- Faith can fail: Luke 22:31-34
- Small faith is all that is needed to do great things: Matthew 17:20
- Faith can grow: Luke 17:5-6

What do these passages tell you or remind you about faith?

With whom do you most identify in the stories? (If you identify with the unbelieving crowd in the passages, this may be the moment God is calling you to cross over into faith in Jesus Christ. If you're studying with a group, ask one of the believers to pray with you as you accept Jesus's sacrifice for your sins. If you're reading on your own, simply pray to Jesus that you realize you're a sinner and you believe he died to pay for your sins. Ask him to lead you into his salvation and to direct you to people who can guide you.)

Write a thought or two about when you realized you wanted to follow Jesus and how following him has affected your life:

Faith Biblical Role Model Ministudy

It helps to know what faith looks like when it's dressed in flesh and blood, doesn't it? For that, we need to see humans exhibiting faith. I take encouragement from the fact that the disciples began with "little" faith. Read Matthew 26:69-75, then Acts 4:1-22.

What is the difference in Peter in these two stories? What factors made this difference?

Read Hebrews 11 and make a list of the men and women of faith listed there. Take special note of 11:32-40. What do these verses tell us about faith as a protection from trial and suffering?

Now choose one or two of the people mentioned here and read their stories in the Old Testament. my favorites are Noah (Genesis 6-9; Hebrews 11:7; 1 Peter 3:20; 2 Peter 2:5), Abraham and Sarah (Genesis 12–25; Romans 4; Galatians 3:6-18; Hebrews 6:13-20), or Gideon (Judges 6–8).

As you read, ask questions.

- How did their faith manifest itself in their lives?
- How did they respond to God? to challenges? to opposition? to disappointments? to blessing?
- How am I like them? How am I different?

Virtue Word Study Exercise

The specific word Peter uses for virtue (*arete*) appears twice in 2 Peter 1:3, 5. Peter uses it also in 1 Peter 2:9, which most versions translate as "praises" or "excellencies," and it's the word Paul uses in Philippians 4:8. List some behaviors or attitudes that most people consider excellent or praiseworthy.

Next, read the following passages and list the behaviors these biblical writers say should be exemplary of Jesus followers.

- Romans 12
- 1 Corinthians 6
- 1 Corinthians 10:23-33
- 2 Corinthians 6
- Galatians 5
- Ephesians 4:17–5:21
- Philippians 2
- Colossians 3:1-17
- 1 Thessalonians 4:1-12
- 2 Thessalonians 3:6-13
- Hebrews 13
- James 1:19-27
- 1 Peter 1:13-17
- 1 John 4:7-21

What effect would it have on your local community if all the believers who lived there behaved according to these passages?

What would it mean to you to live surrounded by Christians who displayed these excellent behaviors?

How can we encourage one another to have the quality of virtue in increasing measure?

What's the difference between the images these verses bring to mind and the way modern media characterize "virtuous" people?

Does it make any sense that a person growing in these characteristics would be boring, stiff, humorless, arrogant, judgmental, or hypocritical?

In what ways do we allow the media to influence our attitudes about our own faith?

How do we let the media play the role of Jack's mother (in the beanstalk story) in our lives, and what would be different if we stopped?

Virtue Biblical Role Model Ministudy

Read the story of Joseph in Genesis 37; 39–46. List the ways in which others wronged Joseph.

How did Joseph respond to these wrongs?

How did Joseph respond to temptation and trial?

How does it appear Joseph responded to power and riches?

Read Genesis 39:23; Proverbs 15:3; Luke 16:10; 2 Chronicles 16:9; and Hebrews 12:1-3. What do these tell us about the value of making right choices even when wronged, even when it feels as though no one is watching?

Choose one of these figures known for making excellent choices in trying times to study deeper: Ruth, Esther, Daniel, Mary, or Joseph, the father of Jesus. When they made the right choices, was the likely outcome clear?

What pressures were on them when they had to make virtuous choices?

Were people around them making choices informed by virtue?

What resulted from their choices for them, for people around them, for the kingdom of God?

What lesson do you learn from these people's lives?

Knowledge Word Study Exercise

Knowledge in Scripture isn't generally a stand-alone quality. Read the following passages and list the purpose, the result, the priority, or the channel for knowledge mentioned in the verses.

- Luke 1:76-79
- Romans 11:33-36
- Romans 15:14
- 1 Corinthians 1:4-5
- 1 Corinthians 13
- 2 Corinthians 2:14-17
- 2 Corinthians 4:6
- 2 Corinthians 6:3-10
- 2 Corinthians 8:7
- 2 Corinthians 10:4-6
- Ephesians 3:14-21
- Philippians 3:8
- Colossians 2:1-3
- 2 Peter 3:18

You will have noted that while love is greater than knowledge, knowledge is still elevated as a priority. Those without a biblical worldview make knowledge and love either/or propositions, but in Christ, they work together to grow us up to full maturity. Consider what you have noted about knowledge as you read these verses. What step will you take to grow in your knowledge of Jesus in the month to come?

Knowledge Biblical Role Model Ministudy

Paul was an intelligent, educated, respected Jewish citizen of Rome when he entered into relationship with Jesus Christ. His knowledge of Jesus didn't puff him up; instead, he became a servant of the church he had once persecuted. Read Acts 15. How did Paul's, Barnabas's, Judas's, and Silas's knowledge serve to strengthen and unite the body of Christ?

Self-Control Word Study Exercise

Read Acts 24:22-27. How did Felix react to Paul's teaching about self-control?

Why are we also prone to react this way when the topic arises?

Read Galatians 5:16-26. Self-control may be intimidating, but how does lack of self-control reveal itself?

How can that help us continue to reach for growth in self-control even when it's challenging or when we suffer failures?

What does it look like to "live by the Spirit" (v. 25)? What role does the Holy Spirit play in encouraging our efforts at self-control?

I like the phrase Paul uses here in the ESV translation: "keep in step with the Spirit" (v. 25 ESV). I walk at a much healthier pace when I walk with my friend Kathy, who is an experienced and fit walker. I also make healthier and holier choices when I'm with others who are trying to do the same. What does it look like, in your life, to "live by the Spirit" and to "keep in step with the Spirit"?

Read Matthew 5:21-30; 2 Corinthians 10:3-6; and James 1:19-27. Consider the qualities we've studied so far and imagine them not as isolated characteristics but as ingredients contributing to spiritual maturity by enhancing one another. Do we see in these passages how faith, virtue, and knowledge can support self-control? What does it look like?

Self-Control Biblical Role Model Ministudy

In the Book of Judges, we find one of God's more colorful creations: the impulsive, headstrong Samson. He's a great study in what happens when a man devoted to God lacks self-control. Read Samson's story in Judges 13–16.

What were the consequences, for himself and for his people, of Samson's consistent lack of self-control?

In the end, God did use Samson to free the Israelites from the Philistines, but he used him from within bondage. This is a great illustration of the fact that God can still use us even as we display a need for growth in these characteristics. Most of us would prefer that he use us while we enjoy the freedom found in following his ways, don't you think? How does the world look upon self-control, and how has that affected your thinking about it?

What are your thoughts on self-control after reading Samson's story?

Steadfastness Word Study Exercise

It's fascinating that John uses the word *steadfastness,* or enduring patience, so often in the Book of Revelation. Read the verses listed here and then summarize why you think God places such a high value on steadfastness in his people: Revelation 1:9; 2:2-3, 9; 3:10; 13:10; 14:12..

Now, work your way back through the other New Testament books and see if your perspective on steadfastness has changed. Write beside each passage what it says about the importance of this virtue:

- Romans 15:4-6:
- 2 Corinthians 1:6-7:

- 2 Corinthians 6:3-10:
- Colossians 1:11:
- 1 Thessalonians 1:3:
- 2 Thessalonians 1:3-4:
- 2 Thessalonians 3:5:
- 1 Timothy 6:11-12:
- 2 Timothy 3:10-13:
- Hebrews 10:36-39:
- Hebrews 12:1-3:
- James 1:2-3:
- James 5:7-11:

Steadfastness Biblical Role Model Ministudy

Many great women of faith have demonstrated patient endurance—certainly Sarah as she waited through decades of barrenness to bear her promised child (Genesis 11–23); Hannah as she petitioned God for her first child (1 Samuel 1); and Abigail, who patiently endured a brutal husband (1 Samuel 25). Many men have endured as well: Hosea (Book of Hosea) patiently endured an unfaithful wife; Job (Book of Job) patiently endured relentless loss; and Daniel (Book of Daniel) was steadfast in prayer through decades of captivity. Choose one of these biblical characters and read his or her story.

What did this person endure?

How did he or she respond to the trials in life?

What was the eventual outcome?

Research how long each one waited for deliverance. What does that say about God's idea of timing?

Godliness Word Study Exercise

This is a great opportunity to see how the characteristics work together. Read 1 Timothy 4. Paul references godliness and reverence in this passage, but he also encourages Timothy to draw on faith, virtue, knowledge, endurance, and steadfastness. These aren't isolated characteristics. They're ingredients that combine to create the mature spiritual condition of not a good Christian, not a perfect Christian, not a magic Christian, but an effective, fruitful Christian. List the places in this passage you see each quality referenced.

Now, read 1 Timothy 6. Again, you'll note that this passage focuses on godliness and reverence, but see if you can find sections that reference the other qualities we've studied so far.

Just as the systems of a living being work together to support the effective living of that being, so these qualities work together in the believer. Read 2 Timothy 3. Why is this characteristic such a challenge to live out in these times?

Did you notice that verse 5 makes reference to the fact that this virtue can be counterfeited? How have you seen this in your experience?

Without faith that would be terrifying, but we are people of faith. This is a strong reminder that God has no desire for us to appear godly. His plan, his heart, his powerful transformative effect is for us actually to be godly.

Godliness Biblical Role Model Ministudy

Two New Testament figures loom large as godly men: Peter and Paul. Choose one to research.

Peter plays a significant role in the Gospels and Acts 1–15, and he authored 1 and 2 Peter. Paul first appears on the scene in Acts 7:58 under his original moniker, Saul. He joined the family and was reborn as Paul in Acts 9. His story continues through the Book of Acts, and he authored at least thirteen books of the New Testament.

If you're short on time, read just a couple of key stories about them. Peter got out of the boat and walked on water with Jesus in Matthew 14. Matthew 26 records his denial of Jesus, and John 21, his restoration. In Acts 4, Peter and John stand before the council in Jerusalem.

Saul witnesses the stoning of Stephen in Acts 7 and persecutes the early church in Acts 8. In Acts 9, Saul meets Jesus on the Damascus Road and becomes a believer, referred to from Acts 13 forward as Paul. If you still believe developing these characteristics will protect you from trials, read Acts 27 and see what Paul endured on his voyage to Rome.

Whichever apostle you choose, make note of every story that reveals one of the character traits to which Peter refers in 2 Peter 1:1-10. Relish any of the stories that reveal that neither of these men was perfect. This isn't a pursuit of perfection but a pursuit of the person of Christ that results in effective living.

Brotherly Affection Word Study Exercise

In 2 Peter 1:7, Peter uses the Greek word *philadelphia,* meaning fraternal affection, brotherly love. List the ways God commands us to actively love one another in the following passages:

- Romans 12:3-21
- 1 Peter 1:13-25
- Hebrews 13:1-17

Apparently, the church in Thessalonica is one to study because, according to Paul in 1 Thessalonians 4:1-12, they had no need for anyone to teach them about brotherly affection because they were so practiced in it. It's worthwhile then to read 1 and 2 Thessalonians in one sitting to get a feel for them and their practices. List their behaviors and consider how you can integrate more of them into your relationships.

Brotherly Affection Biblical Role Model Ministudy

Research one of these biblical figures who exhibited fervent brotherly affection: Follow the story of Jonathan and David in 1 Samuel 18–31. Read the sweet, short story of Dorcas is in Acts 9:36-42. John refers to himself as "the disciple whom he loved." Read references to him in Jesus's final days on earth to see what actions resulted from their brotherly affection as Jesus endured the cross (John 19:26; 20:2; 21:7; 21:20).

Love Word Study Exercise

Read 1 Corinthians 13 and make a list of people you love. Think about each person and ask yourself if you offer them the love described in 1 Corinthians 13:4-7. Read 1 John 4:7-21. Consider the list of giants you made at the start of this book. What does love look like in the face of those giants?

How can God's perfect love cast fear out of those circumstances?

In light of this passage, what should we consider before we casually state we love God but don't love his church?

Love Biblical Role Model Ministudy

Jesus is love. He is a living, breathing study in love. If we want to know what love looks like in the flesh, we have only to look to Jesus. Read one of the Gospels (Matthew, Mark, Luke, or John) in one sitting. As you read, make a list of the action verbs ascribed to Jesus. What can they tell us about how love acts?

Read a separate Gospel each week for four weeks and do the same each time. How does Jesus exemplify love?

Hints and Helps for Using This Book Individually and in Small Groups

My vision for this book is that individuals will benefit from reading it alone, but it is also easy to use with small groups, Sunday school classes, Bible studies, and leadership retreats. I've referenced many Bible passages rather than quote them to encourage readers to open God's Word themselves and read each passage in context.

Individuals or One-on-One Discipleship

It's devised to be easy for solitary study. It's also a great book for use in one-on-one discipleship. Assign one chapter per week and meet to discuss the questions over coffee. Proceed at whatever pace makes sense for each individual.

Sixteen-, Ten-, Eight-, or Six-Week Studies

The book is divided into three sections and sixteen chapters. It can be covered in sixteen weeks (one chapter per week) with a natural division at the halfway mark between Part 2 and Part 3. Many small-group leaders enjoy doing eight weeks, then another eight weeks.

It's profitable to cover the first eight chapters as a small-group study and then encourage individuals to complete the next eight weeks on their own. Invite everyone back after those eight weeks for an evening to discuss what they've learned. Or enjoy a daylong workshop on the eight characteristics so participants can share ideas they discovered through their individual study times.

Some groups will enjoy starting the study with a daylong retreat. The material in chapters 1–8 can be covered in one day (chapters 1–4 in the morning, 5–8 in the afternoon). Start and end the retreat with a time of worship or follow dinner with a showing of a favorite, age-appropriate film version of "Jack and the Beanstalk." Follow the retreat with an eight-week small group or Sunday school study using chapters 9–16.

The entire book can be covered in eight weeks by doing two chapters per week or by having participants read one chapter from Parts 1 or 2 along with one characteristic section from Part 3 each week.

If need be, it can also be covered in six weeks by doing chapters 1–4 for week one and chapters 5–8 for week two and then covering the next eight chapters two per week.

If you have ten weeks, I recommend following an eight-week format but allow one week to discuss the giants facing group participants or your church. Pray about them and brainstorm ways that developing these eight characteristics can work against these giants. Allow another week to examine the way your church or the community you're trying to reach for Christ cries out for beans. Brainstorm creative ways to reach them for Christ with this new understanding.

Retreats

Ministry teams may enjoy studying this book before leading the church to study it. Assign the book to be read prior to a weekend leadership retreat. Cover the first four chapters Friday night and share the list of giants facing your ministry team or congregation. Cover the second four chapters Saturday morning. Examine the ways your congregation, as well as those in your community you're attempting to reach, cry out for beans. For Saturday afternoon, break into either four or eight groups to cover each of the eight characteristics, allowing time to share at the end. Compile lists of activities to encourage growth in these areas as a ministry team and as a congregation. Saturday night, worship together and enjoy a showing of a "Jack and the Beanstalk" film.

Sunday morning, pray together over all you've learned and commit to growing in these qualities and encouraging your church to grow as well.

This material will work well with teen or young adult retreats, too. Present the concepts introduced in Parts 1 and 2 using the first part of the "Jack and the Beanstalk" story and the chapter questions. Allow plenty of time for young people to list the giants they face and to examine how their culture cries out for beans. Use the retreat as a launch pad to study the next eight chapters over eight weeks. Make it a challenge for these young people to identify ways their peers cry out for beans through the arts during those eight weeks.

Resources

You'll find a section on resources and activity ideas on my website at www.loriroeleveld.com. As you discover resources or ideas for ways to use this book, let me know through my contact page, and I'll add them to the list (crediting you, of course). This way we can all grow together.

Acknowledgments

If God works through the words of this book in any reader's heart, then these loved ones also own a portion of that for their labors of love in the name of Jesus.

To my readers, for inspiring, challenging, and encouraging every word so that I work to offer you my best every day in Jesus' name. For those of you who volunteered to be early readers of *Jesus and the Beanstalk*, your feedback was invaluable. You have my deepest thanks.

To Ramona Richards, author and editor extraordinaire, for believing in my voice. To the team at Abingdon—Holly Halverson, Dawn Woods, Deanna Nelson, Susan Cornell, the sales and design teams, and Susan Salley, among others, for embracing this book and sharing the vision.

To Les Stobbe, for your enduring labor of love on my behalf, your prayers, and for Rita. To Jerry B. Jenkins, for your investment in me, for your example, and for setting the bar high. To my writing family at Blue Ridge Mountains Christian Writers Conference for our annual glimpse of glory. To Eddie Jones for sacrificing to provide me a launchpad.

To Jim Rubart for helping me read my label (and for *Jacob Palmer*) and to Darci for the voice mail that sealed our friendship. To the warrior women writers of The Light Brigade—it's an honor to count myself in your number. To the Prayer is the Work team who intercede for every word I write and speak, to God be the glory, my co-laborers in God's great field. To the friends who cheer me on and help me see the forest when the trees are in the way, especially, Alton and Becky, Aaron, Kathy and Bruce, Cherrilyn, Arline and Jim, and Edie and Kirk.

To my church family at First Baptist Church of Hope Valley for keeping me grounded, and especially Micki, for all the meals you cooked as I wrote! To Mr. James Campbell for being my father in the faith all those years ago.

To my mom and dad, Fred and Sylvia Stanley, for laying down your lives for me every day in these past years, for all the prayers, laughter, meals, Patriots games, and unconditional love that sustained me as I learned to slay giants. To my brother, Loren, for living all the best stories.

To Hannah, for being fearless and strong in Christ as you tell your story, and to Zack, for continually fueling my love of myths and fairy tales. To you both for letting me write about our shared adventures. To Andrew, thank you for loving my girl so well and to Jess for inspiring my son to be his best self. Welcome to the family.

To Rob, you believe in me and demonstrate that in a thousand ways every day. I'm glad we stuck out the tough times because our love is truly richer now than when our adventure first began. Here's to continuing our happily ever after until He comes…

Notes

Why Atheists Fear Fairy Tales

1. Richard Dawkins on fairy tales: "I think it's rather pernicious to inculcate into a child a view of the world which includes supernaturalism" (Ian Johnston, *Independent,* 5 June 2014, www.independent.co.uk/news/people/professor-richard-dawkins-claims-fairy-tales-are-harmful-to-children-9489287.html).

2. A Long Line of Giant-Killers

1. C. S. Lewis, "On Three Ways of Writing for Children" (1952), in *Of Other Worlds,* ed. Walter Hooper (New York: Harcourt Brace Jovanovich, 1966), 25.

2. C. S. Lewis, dedication in *The Lion, the Witch, and the Wardrobe* (London: Geoffrey Bles, 1950).

4. Where Peter Spills the Beans

1. Lori Stanley Roeleveld, *Running from a Crazy Man (and Other Adventures Traveling with Jesus)* (Raleigh, NC: Lighthouse Publishing of the Carolinas, 2014), 19–20.

6. Surviving the Famine

1. "The State of the Bible: Six Trends for 2014," Barna, April 8, 2014, www.barna.org/barna-update/culture/664-the-state-of-the-bible-6-trends-for-2014#.VdyETPlViko.

2. Alizeh Kohari, "Who, What, Why: What Is a Famine?" BBC News, July 20, 2011, www.bbc.com/news/world-us-canada-14199080.

3. Evan Andrews, "6 World War II Propaganda Broadcasters," August 13,

2013, History.com, www.history.com/news/history-lists/6-world-war-ii-propa ganda-broadcasters.

8. How the World Cries Out for Beans

1. Jesse Carey, "15 Augustine Quotes That Helped Shape Modern Christian Thought," *Relevant Magazine*, August 28, 2014, www.relevantmagazine .com/god/15-augustine-quotes-helped-shape-modern-christian-thought# QKbJrdyRmrDf4dJX.99.

9. Faith Buries the Beans

1. James Strong, *A Complete Bible Reference Study Library (4 in 1), s.v. pistis* (Strong's no. g4102) and *peithos* (Strong's no. g3982) (Bestbooks 2015), Kindle edition.

2. Daniel W. Whittle, "I Know Whom I Have Believed" (1883).

3. James Strong, *A Complete Bible Reference Study Library (4 in 1), s.v. lagchano* (Strong's no. g2975) (Bestbooks 2015), Kindle edition.

4. Joshua Ratner, "What Does 'Dayenu' Mean Today?" April 1, 2014, My Jewish Learning, www.myjewishlearning.com/rabbis-without-borders/ what-does-dayenu-mean-today/.

10. Virtue from the Ground Up

1. James Strong, *A Complete Bible Reference Study Library (4 in 1)*, s.v. *arete* (Strong's no. g703) (Bestbooks 2015), Kindle edition.

11. Knowledge for the Climb

1. Ed Stetzer, "Dumb and Dumber: How Biblical Illiteracy Is Killing Our Nation," *Charisma Magazine*, October 9, 2014, www.charismamag.com/life /culture/21076-dumb-and-dumber-how-biblical-illiteracy-is-killing-our-nation.

12. Self-Control for Repeat Offenders

1. "Thousands of Christians Form Human Shield to Protect Church," April 7, 2014, Charisma News, www.charismanews.com/world/43416-thousands -of-christians-form-human-shield-to-protect-church.

2. Charlene Aaron, "Hostage Kayla Mueller's Family Releases Letter She Wrote," February 11, 2015, CBN News, www1.cbn.com/cbnnews/world/2015/February/US-Woman-held-by-ISIS-Dead-Parents-Confirm/.

3. "Charlie Hebdo Attack: Three Days of Terror," January 14, 2015, BBC News, www.bbc.com/news/world-europe-30708237.

4. Edwin Mora, "Girl Says She Refused Boko Haram's Demand to Be Suicide Bomber to Enter Paradise," Breitbart.com, December 26, 2014, www.breitbart.com/national-security/2014/12/26/girl-says-she-refused-boko-harams-demand-to-be-suicide-bomber-to-enter-paradise/.

13. Steadfastness in Slippery Times

1. Andy Snyder, "Here are Four Traits That Every Good Fisherman Has," June 20, 2008, *The York Dispatch,* http://archive.yorkdispatch.com/ci_9646063.

14. Godliness for Giant-Killers

1. Definition retrieved from www.blueletterbible.org/lang/lexicon/lexicon.cfm?Strongs=G2150&t=KJV, s.v. *godliness* (Strong's no. g2150).

2. J. R. R. Tolkien, "All That Is Gold Does Not Glitter," in *The Fellowship of the Ring* (Boston: Houghton Mifflin, 1987).

3. Latin Dictionary Online, s.v. *coram*. www.latin-dictionary.org/coram.

15. Brotherly Affection with Backbone

1. James Strong, *A Complete Bible Reference Study Library (4 in 1)*, s.v. *philadelphia* (Strong's no. g5360) (Bestbooks 2015), Kindle edition.

2. "Rebels Kill 30 in Church Raid in Central African Republic," *Los Angeles Times,* May 28, 2014, www.latimes.com/world/africa/la-fg-rebels-kill-30-central-african-republic-20140528-story.html.

3. Faith Karimi and Mohammed Osman, "Sudanese Woman Sentenced to Death for her Christianity Gives Birth in Prison," CNN, May 29, 2014, www.cnn.com/2014/05/27/world/africa/sudan-christian-woman-apostasy/.

4. "Eradication of Christianity in Northern Cameroon," Open Doors, May 23, 2014, www.opendoorsusa.org/take-action/pray/tag-prayer-updates-post/eradication-of-christianity-in-northern-cameroon/.

5. "China: Provision and Prayer," Voice of the Martyrs, May 20, 2014, www.persecution.com/public/newsroom.aspx?story_ID=%3d363834&featuredstory_ID=%3d343431.

6. "North Korea Christian Persecution," North Korean Christians.com, www.northkoreanchristians.com/persecution-christian.html.

16. Love That Invites and Incites

1. "A word or way of speaking or behaving which shows that a person belongs to a particular group." Merriam-Webster Online Dictionary, www.merriam-webster.com/dictionary/shibboleth.

2. "A sharp, upward slap to the back of the head given to someone acting blaringly stupid. Originated from Special Agent Gibbs from *NCIS* who employs this maneuver often." Urban Dictionary, October 7, 2005, www.urbandictionary.com/define.php?term=Gibbs-slap.